Early Childhood Basic Skills Activities

by
Sherrill B. Flora

illustrated by
Duane Barnhart

(A Compilation of the Teaching Tablets Series)

Publishers
T.S. Denison & Company, Inc.
Minneapolis, Minnesota 55431

T.S. DENISON & Co., INC.

Standard Book Number: 513-02047-0
Early Childhood Basic Skills Activities
Copyright © 1991 by the T.S. Denison Company, Inc.
Minneapolis, Minnesota 55431

INTRODUCTION

PENCIL FUN - This chapter provides first experiences with using pencils and crayons. Simple Mazes, tracing and connecting the dots. Teach directionality and a variety of strokes. Children will be thrilled with the built-in success of learning pencil skills with the Pencil Fun chapter.

SHAPES - Thios chapter teaches six shapes. Children learn to draw shapes, discriminate the shapes in objects and may learn to read the shape words. All the shapes are taught through tracing, coloring, cutting and pasting activities.

COLORS - This chapter teaches eight colors. Children learn to name the colors, write the color words and read color words, through the fun of coloring, cutting and pasting.

READINESS SKILLS AND CONCEPTS - This chapter provides the teacher with activities that will promote an understanding of basic concepts, readiness skills, classifying, patterning, sequencing, and thinking skills. All of the activities are presented through interesting and creative fine motor activities.

ALPHABET - Children will learn to recognize and identify upper and lower case alphabet letters, along with printing the letters and becoming familiar with beginning consonant sounds. This chapter is organized in alphabetical sequence.

NUMBERS - In this chapter numbers one through ten are taught. Children learn to rote count, identify written numbers and to match numbers to a cooresponding group of objects. Review and enrichment activities are included.

CUT, COLOR AND PASTE PUZZLES - The floor puzzles, form puzzles, small puzzles and story puzzles in this chapter will delight the children! The puzzle pieces can be pasted on paper to create puzzle pictures. Children love to put together puzzles and work with their hands. This chapter combines both interests.

SAFETY - The activities in this chapter are provided to teach and increase a child's awareness of potentially dangerous situations. Each page in this chapter represents a different safety rule. Children learn how to be "safe" through non-threatening, creative activities.

PLACES TO GO - This chapter provides twelve background pages of places that children know. Each background has an accessory page filled with objects and people that belong in that particular scene.

CONTENTS

Pencil Fun

WE ARE HUNGRY!

Help us find our food!

Draw a line from the animal to its food. Color the animals. Can you name them?

SURPRISES!

Help the children find their surprises!

Draw a line from the child to the surprise.
Color the children and their surprises.

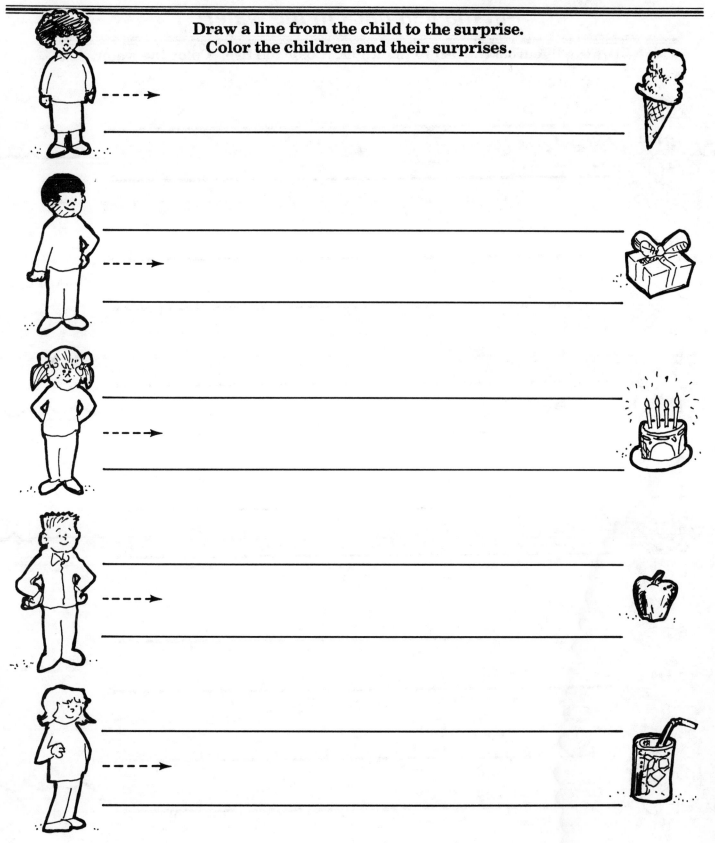

FISH LIVE IN THE WATER

Put the fish back in the water!

Draw a line from the fish to the water. Color the fish. Color the water.

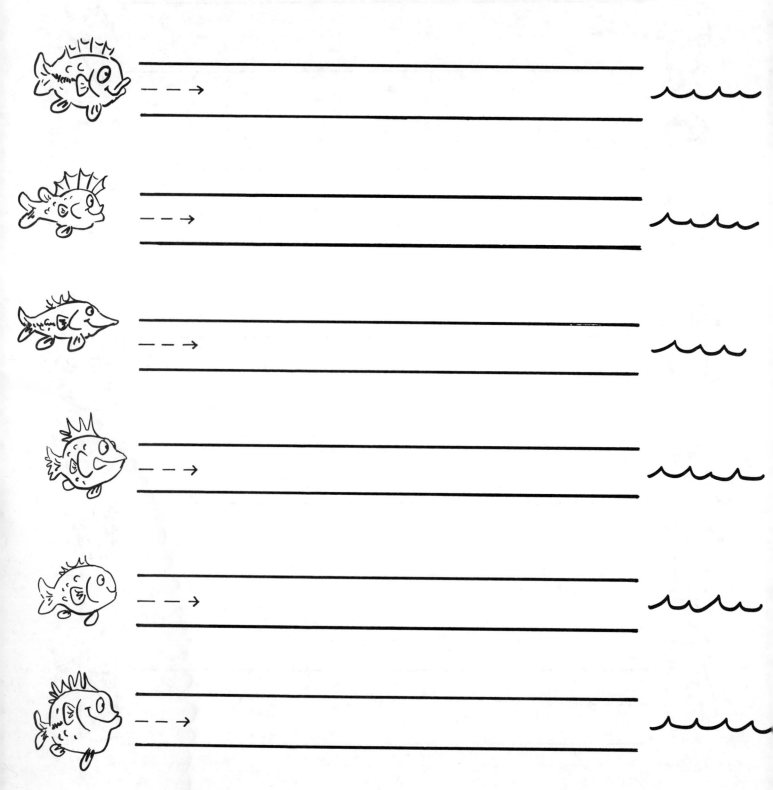

BULLS-EYE

Shoot the arrow into the target!

Draw a line from the arrow to the target.

BEES MAKE HONEY
Help each bee find his flower.

Draw straight lines. Color the bees. Color the flowers.

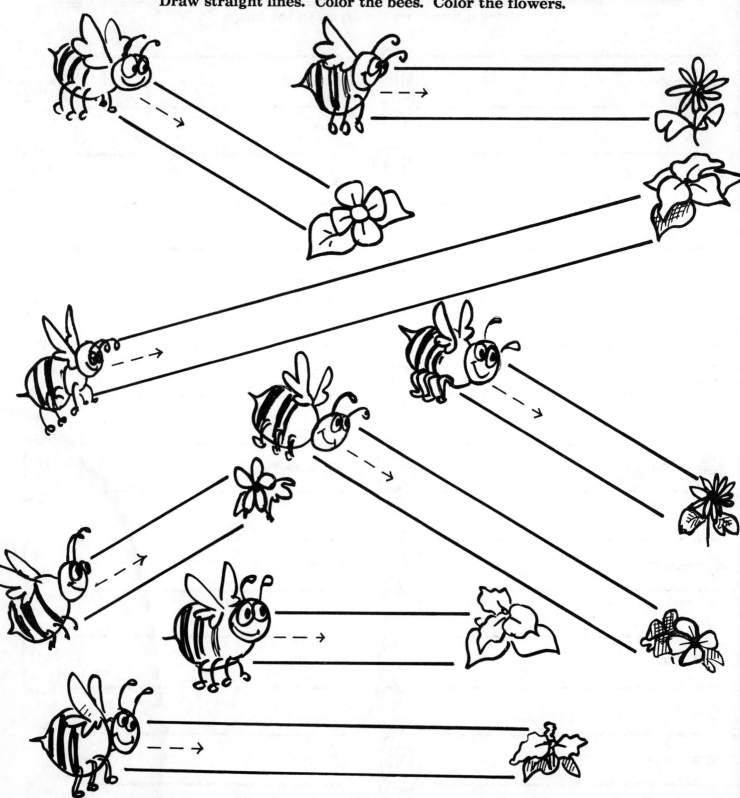

DRIVE ON THE ROAD

Stay on the road and stop at the stop sign.

Drive each vehicle on the road to the stop sign.

T.S. Denison & Co., Inc./Early Childhood Basic Skills Activities

OUTER SPACE

Help each rocket find its planet.

**Draw a line between each rocket and planet.
Stay on course so the rockets won't crash.**

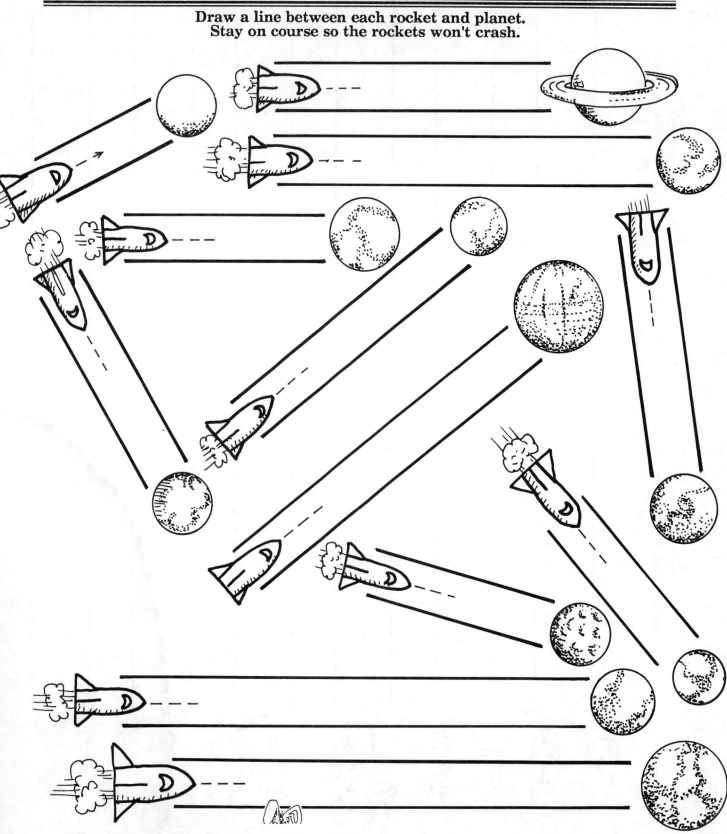

THE FOUR SEASONS

Match the season to the object that people use during that season.

Don't stray off the path. Can you name the seasons? Color the pictures.

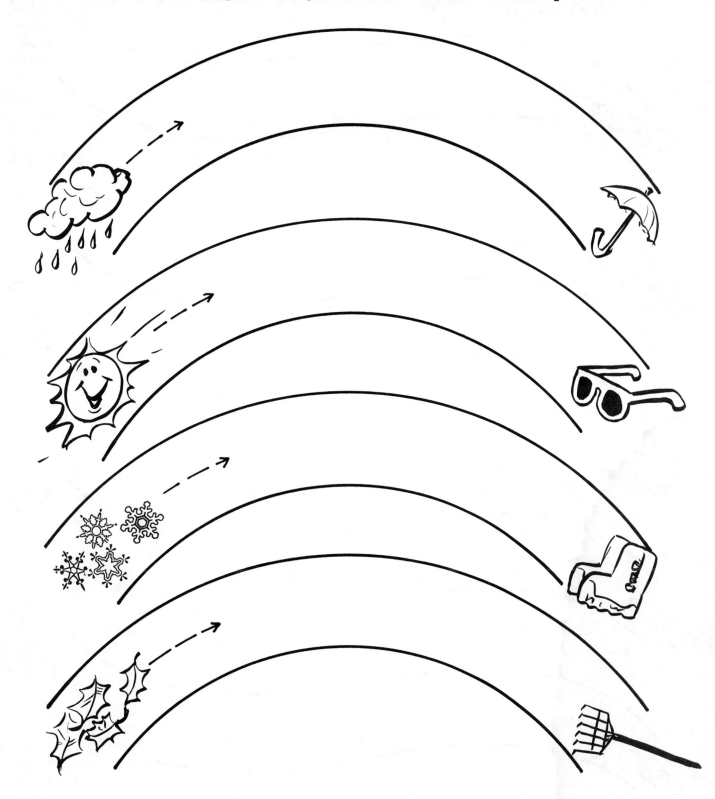

I AM GOING TO BE A BUTTERFLY

Help the caterpillars turn into butterflies.

Start at the caterpillars and draw curved lines to the butterflies.
Color the picture.

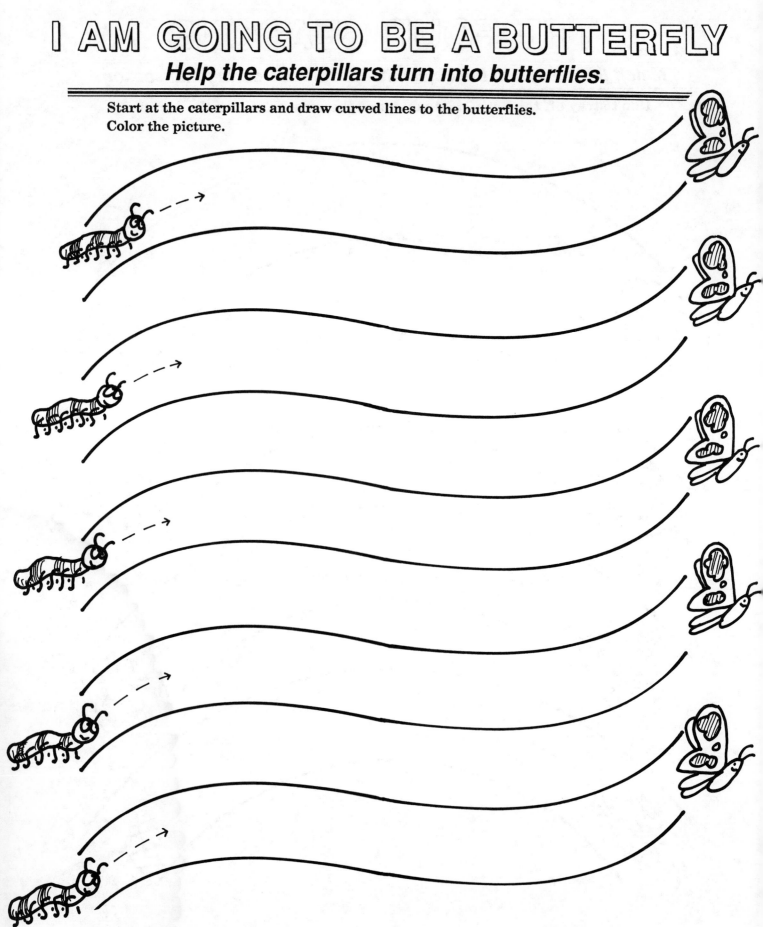

MICE LOVE CHEESE!

Help the mice get to the cheese.

Be careful when you draw the lines.
The mice don't want to get caught in any of the traps.

ANTS LOVE A PICNIC!

Help the ants sneak through the grass to get to the picnic baskets.
Don't get lost in the grass!

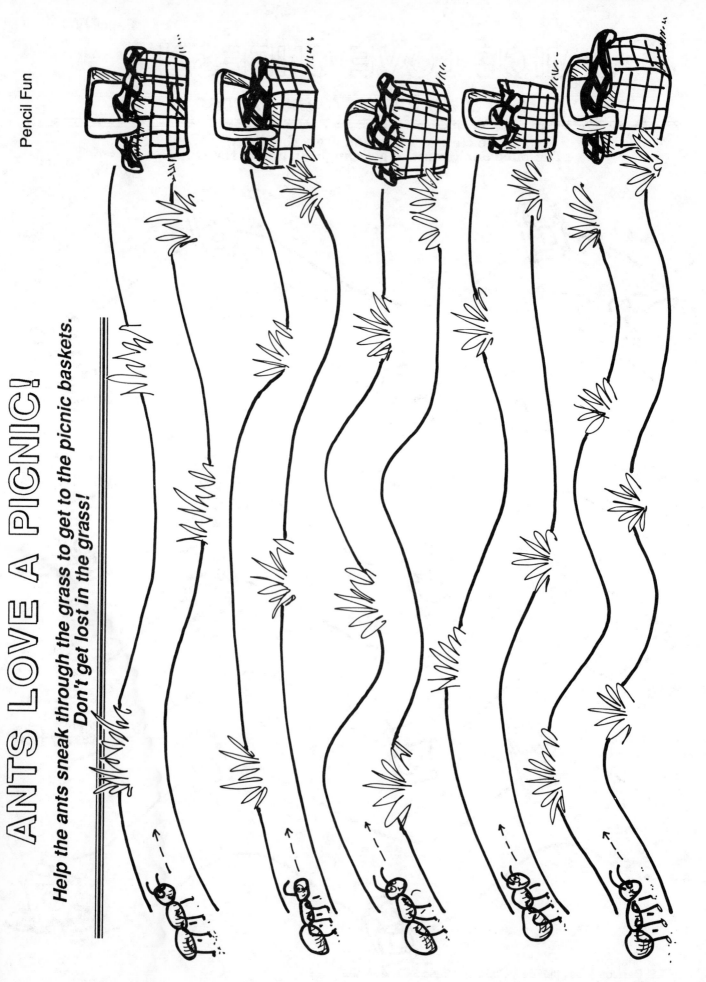

T.S. Denison & Co., Inc./Early Childhood Basic Skills Activities

By the time you get to this page, you should be drawing very well with a pencil. Now draw curved lines from the pencils to the paper.

Make a happy face in the square for doing such a GOOD JOB!

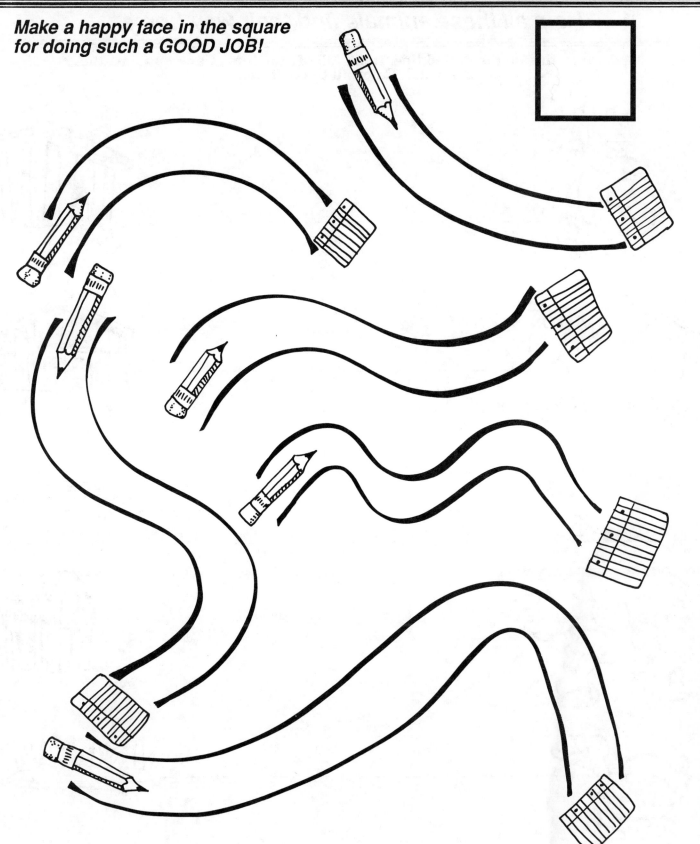

ANIMAL HOMES

Help all these animals find their way home.

Draw a line on the dotted line. Don't fall off the line. Can you name the animals? Color all the pictures.

SLIDING IN THE WINTER

Slide down the hill with your pencil. Don't fall off the hill.

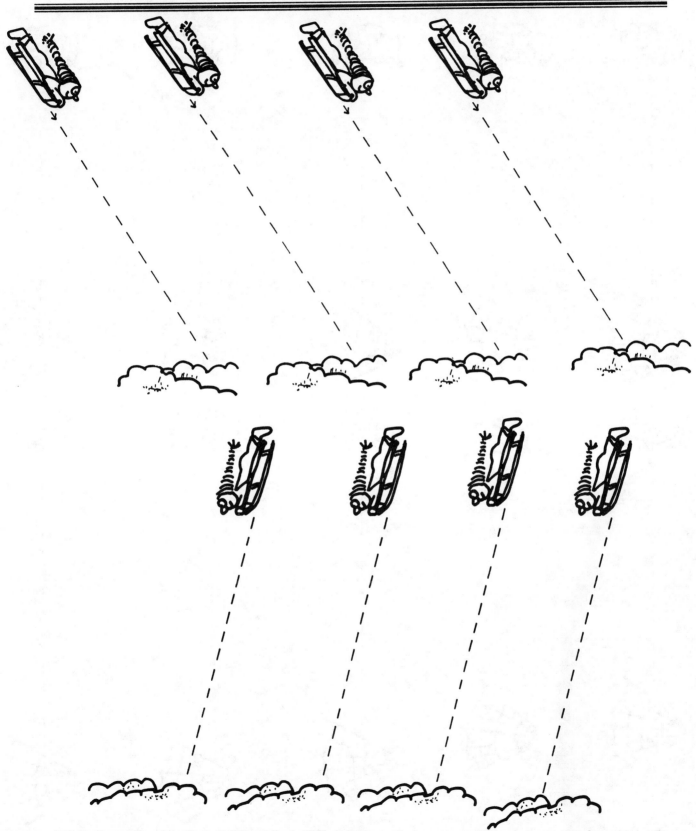

SPIDERS
The spiders want to go home to their webs.

Use your pencil and help the spiders down the dotted line to their webs.

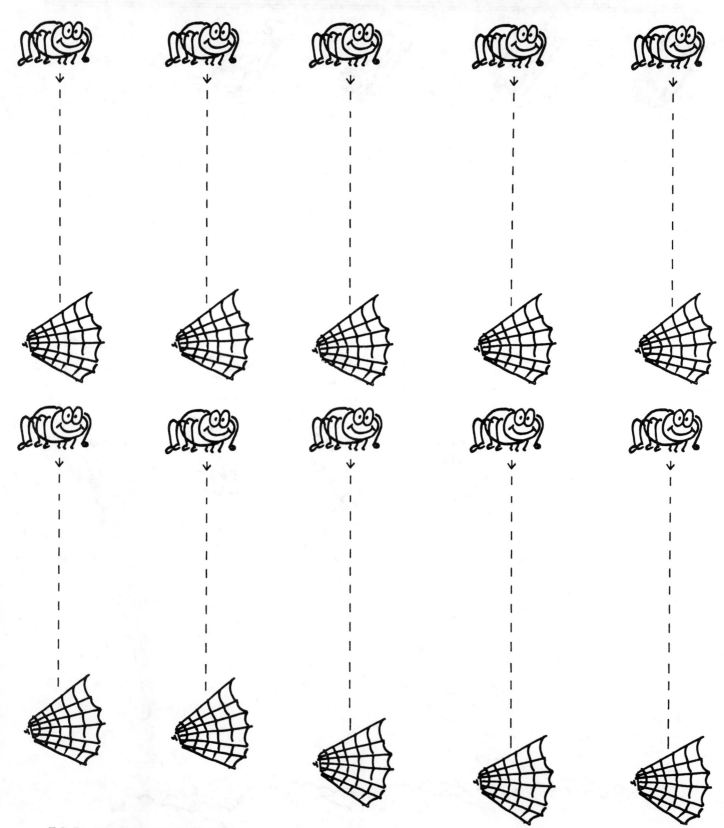

SHOW OFF!
You can draw terrific lines now!

Draw some straight lines.
Give yourself happy faces in both squares

THE ANIMALS ARE LOST
Use your pencil to help the animals get home

Can you name the animals? Do you know where they are? Color the pictures.

SLITHER SNAKES

Slither through the grass with the snakes.

Get each snake to the end of its path. Color each snake a different color.

T.S. Denison & Co., Inc./Early Childhood Basic Skills Activities

BALLOONS
These balloons need strings.

Give each balloon a string. Draw nice straight lines.

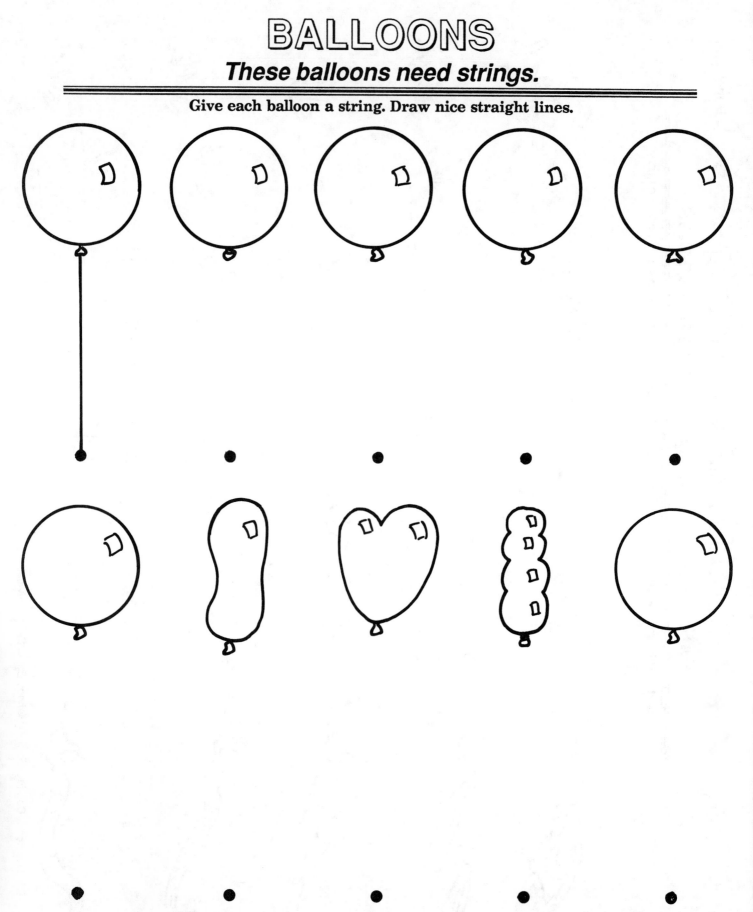

FLOWER POTS
Flowers have petals, stems and leaves.

Draw all the stems. Draw leaves on the stems. Color the flowers.

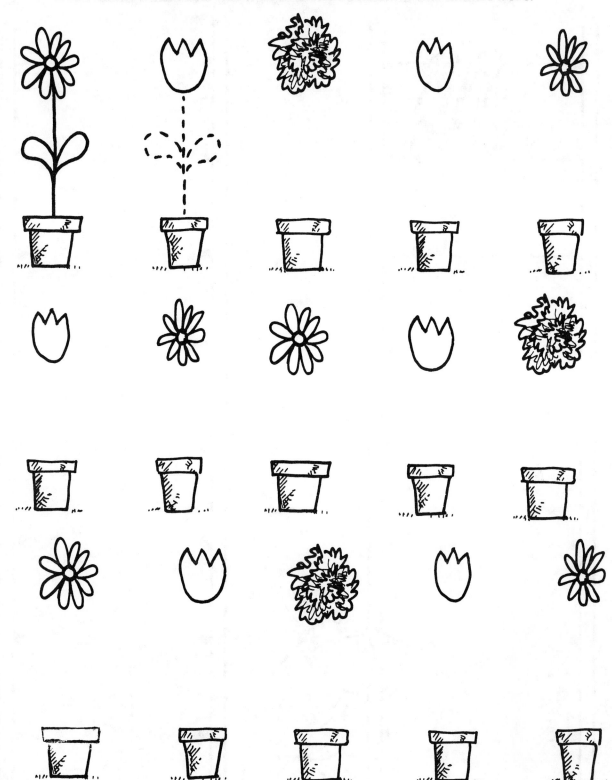

FIRE FIGHTERS
Fire Fighters climb ladders.

Finish the ladders so the fire fighters can climb them.

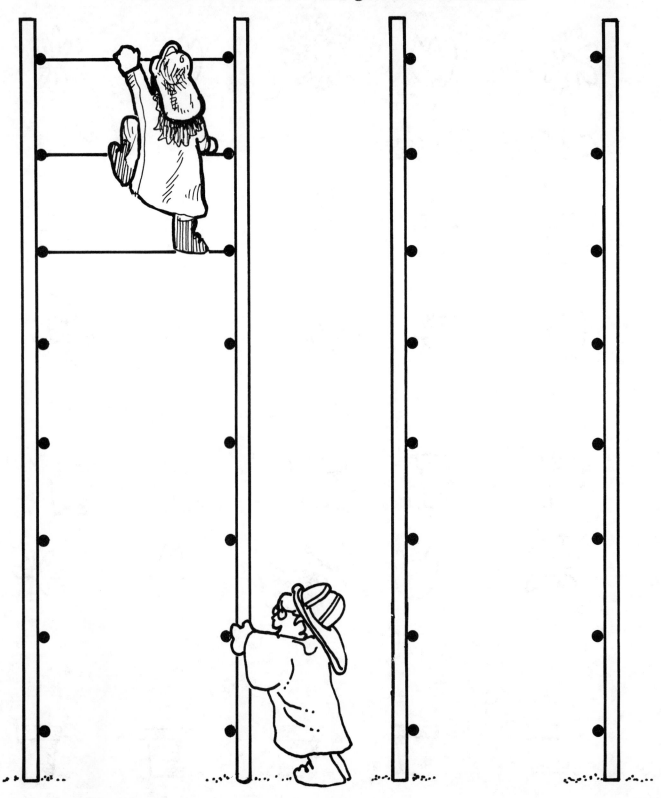

ROLLER SKATING

Skate around the roller rink with your pencil.

Don't go out of the rink. You have just made circles.
Give yourself a happy face inside each circle.

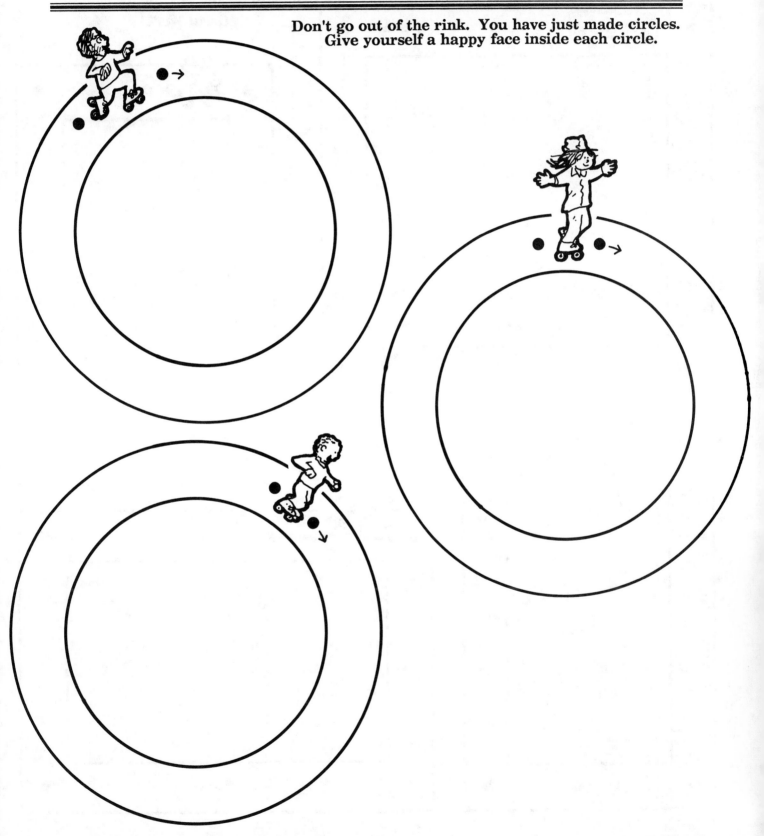

Let's Go Around the Block!

Draw straight lines. Stop at each dot.

Great Work!

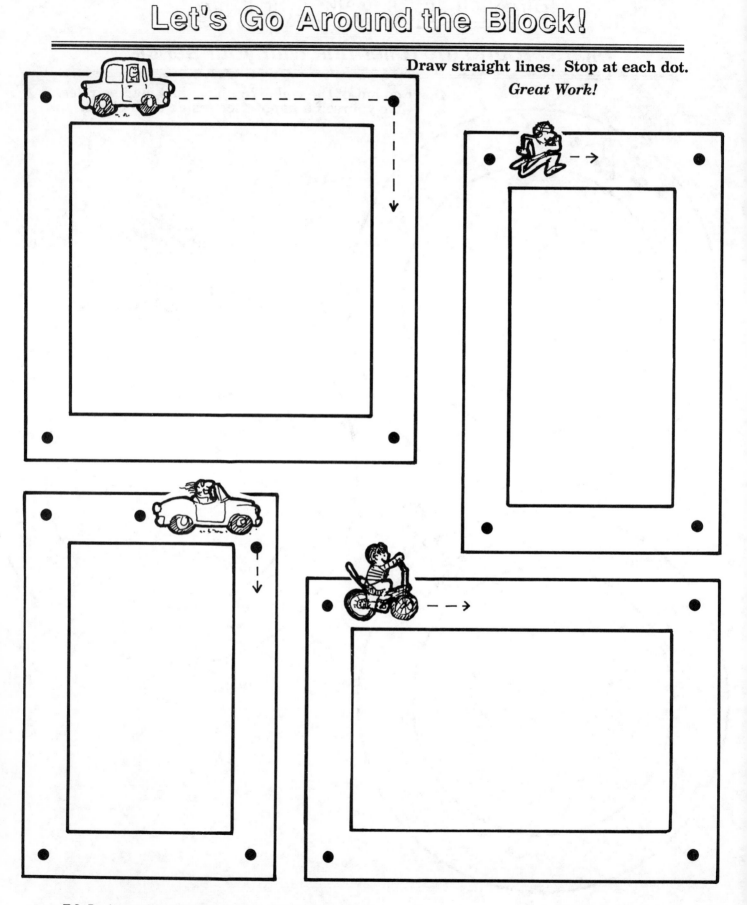

Child's Name

Date

is learning to use a pencil.

show off your great work!!!!

Shapes

○CIRCLES○

Name_____

These are circles.
Trace them and color them.

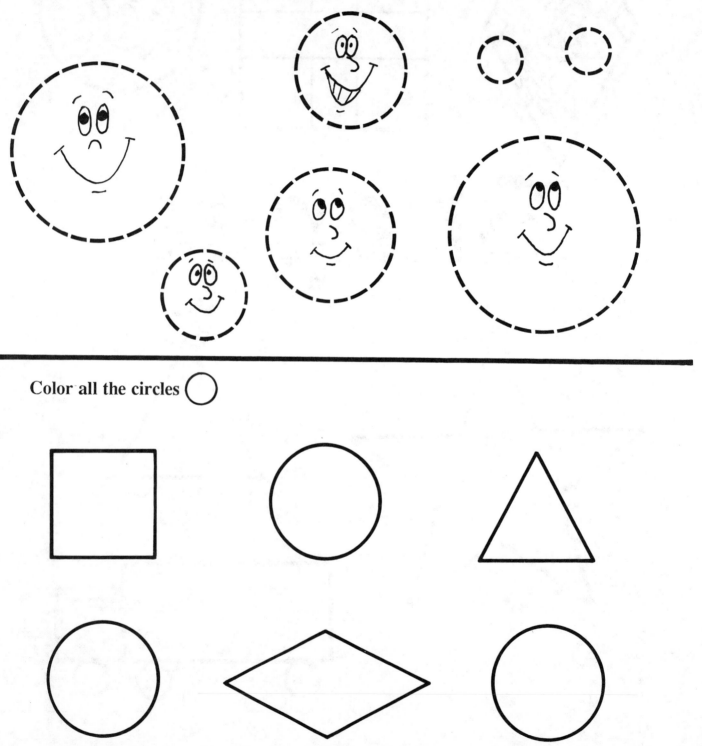

Color all the circles ○

CIRCLES

Name_____

Color the objects that
are shaped like circles. ◯

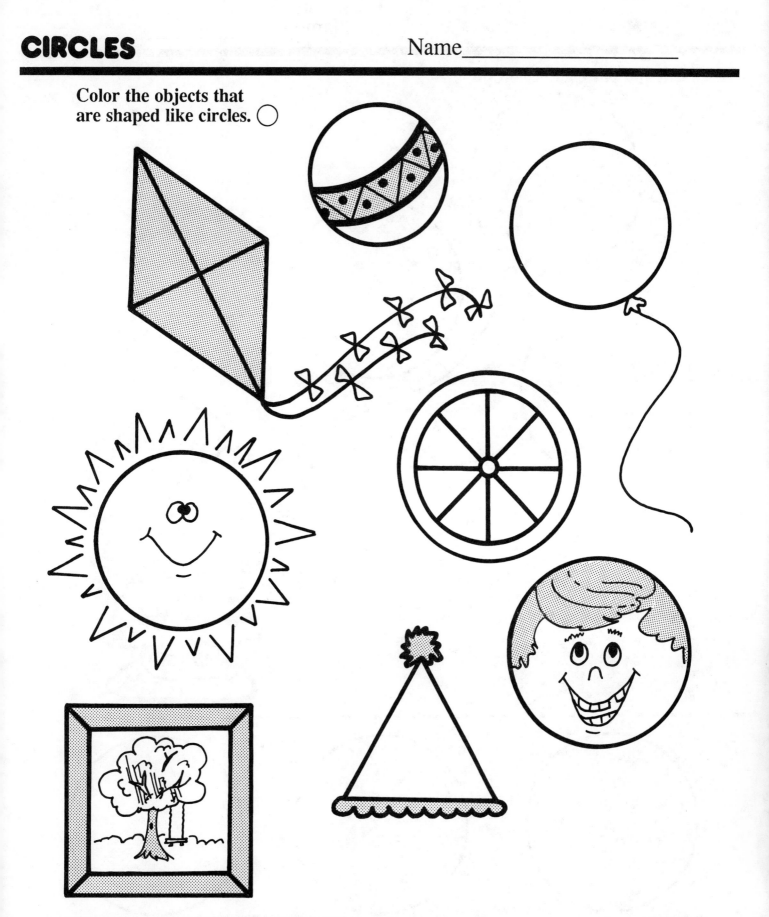

CIRCLES

Name_____

Cut and paste and color

SQUARES

Name_____

These are squares.
Trace them and color them.

Color all the squares.

SQUARES

Name_____

Color the objects that
are shaped like squares. ☐

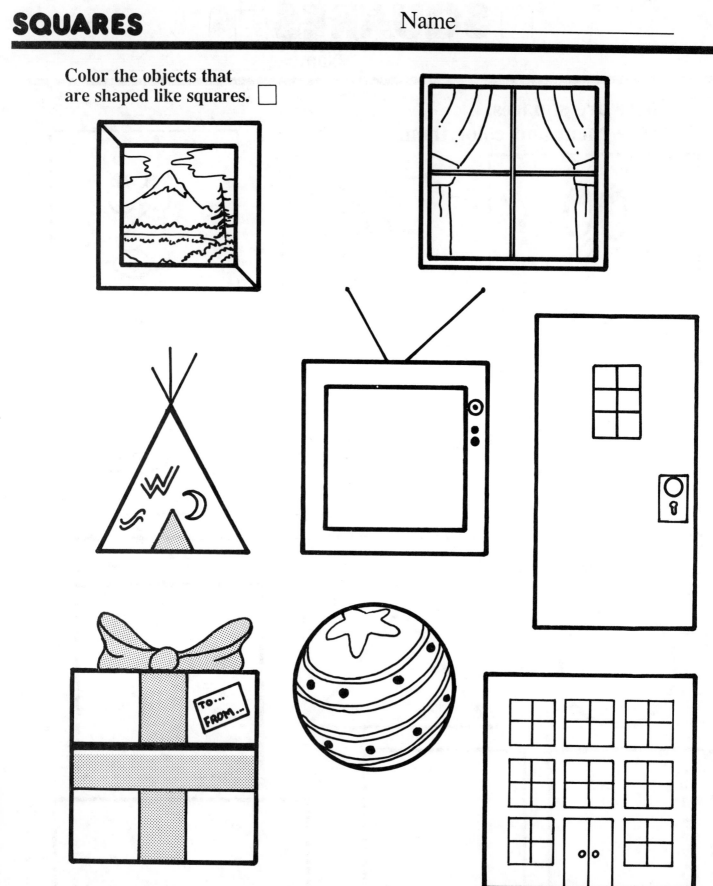

○ CIRCLE AND SQUARE □

Name_____

Cut and paste and color.

△ TRIANGLES △

Name_____

These are triangles.
Trace them and color them.

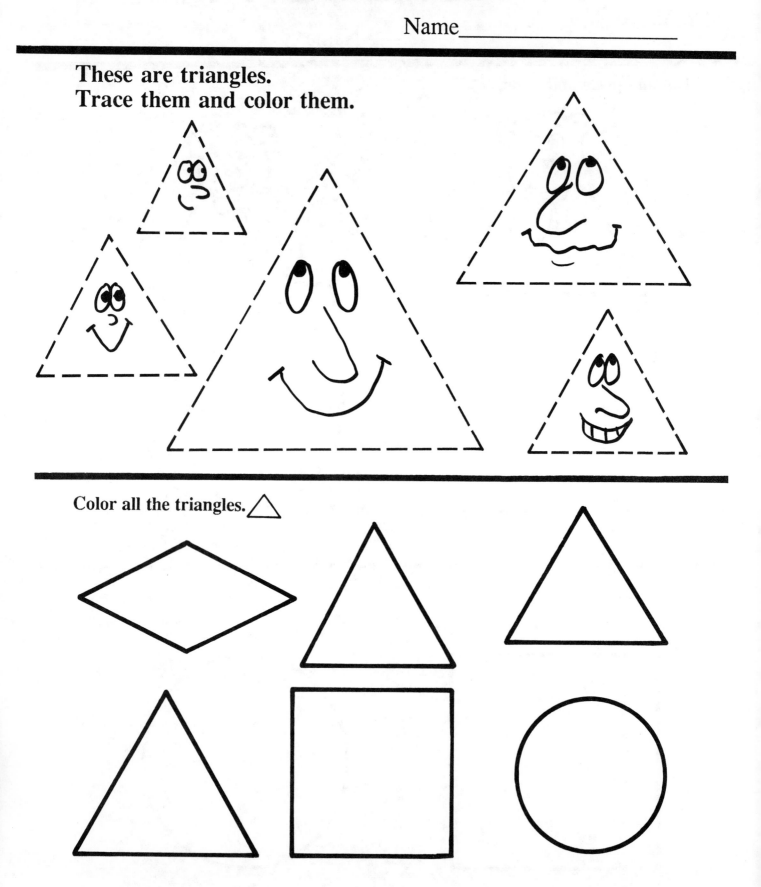

Color all the triangles. △

TRIANGLES

Name_____

Color the objects that
are shaped like triangles. △

□ SQUARE AND TRIANGLE △

Name_____

Cut and paste and color.

CIRCLES - SQUARES - TRIANGLES

○   □   △

Name_____

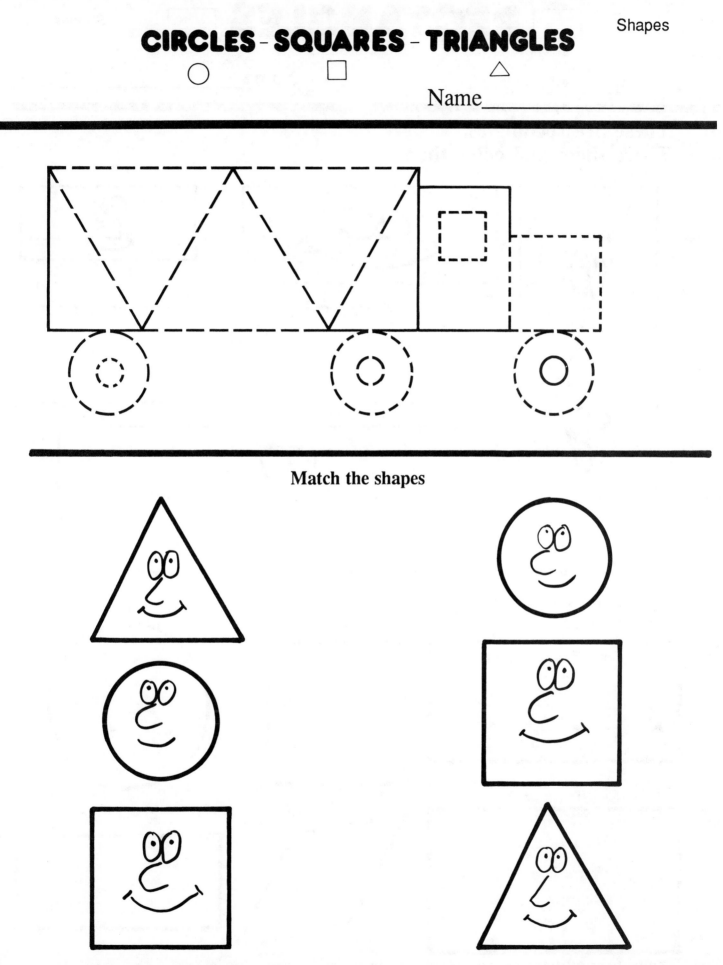

Match the shapes

Name_____

These are rectangles.
Trace them and color them.

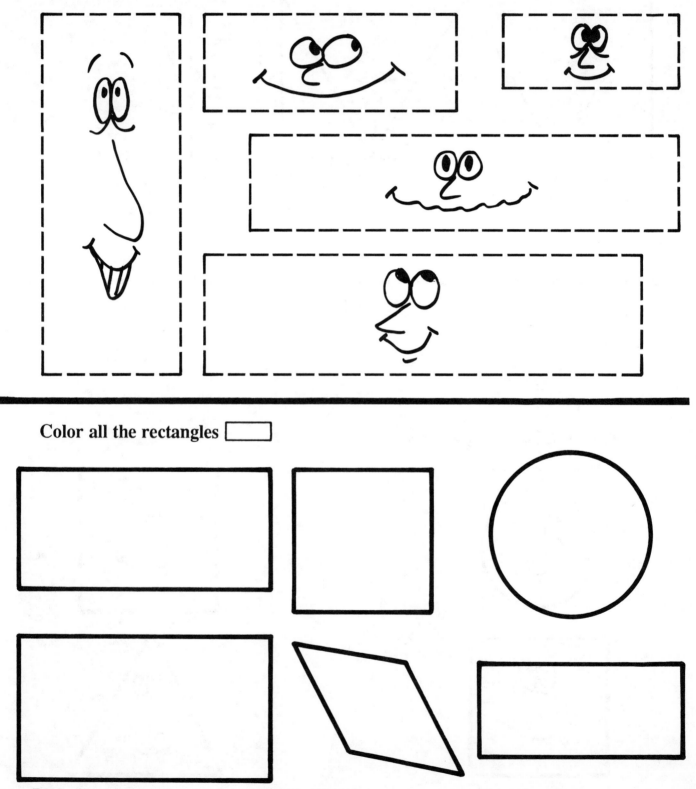

Color all the rectangles □

RECTANGLES

Name_____

**Color the objects that
are shaped like rectangles.** ▭

△ TRIANGLE AND RECTANGLE ▭

Name_____

Cut, paste and color.

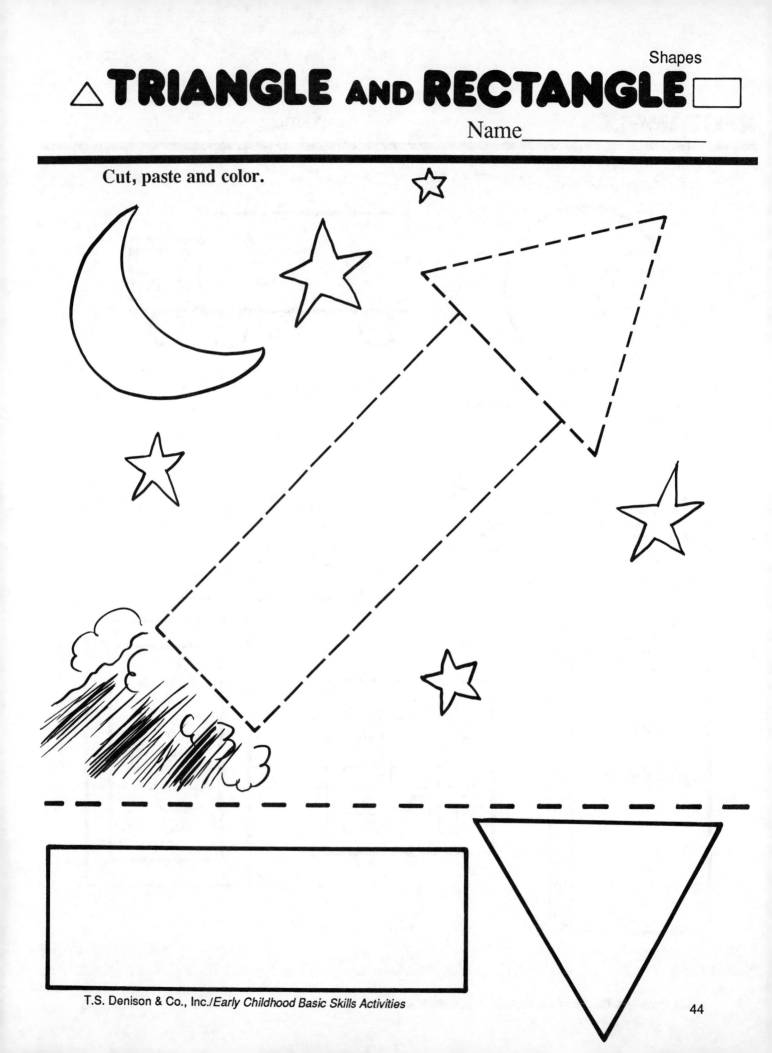

◇ DIAMONDS ◇

Name_____

These are diamonds.
Trace them and color them.

Color the diamonds.

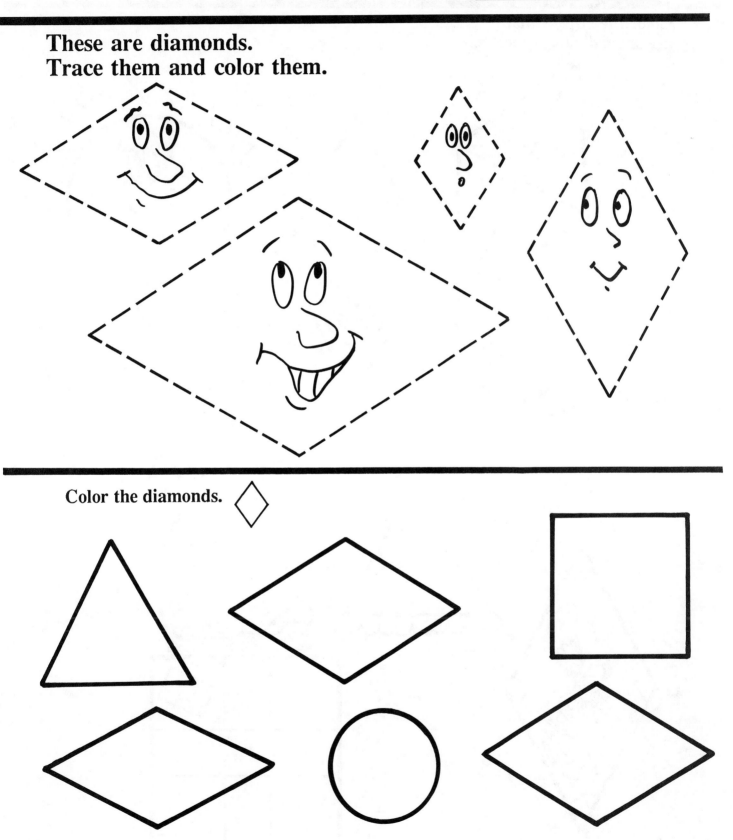

DIAMONDS

Name_____

Color the objects that are shaped like diamonds.

▭ RECTANGLE AND DIAMOND ◇

Name_____

Cut and paste and color.

☆ **STARS** ☆

Name_____

These are stars.
Trace them and color them.

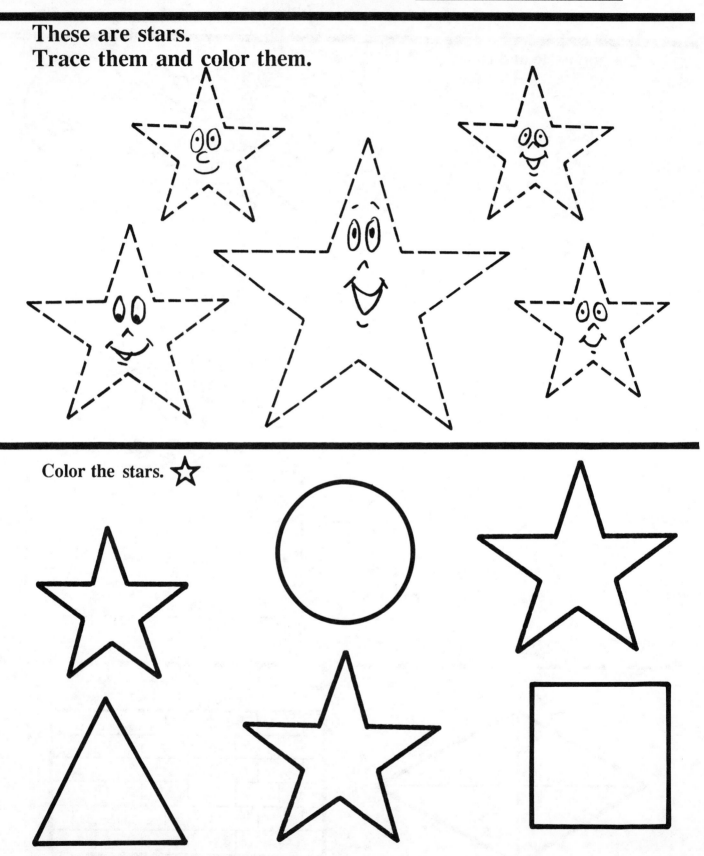

Color the stars. ☆

STARS

Name_____

Color the objects that
are shaped like stars. ☆

◇ DIAMOND AND STAR ☆ Shapes

Name_____

Cut and paste.

RECTANGLE DIAMOND STAR

Name_____

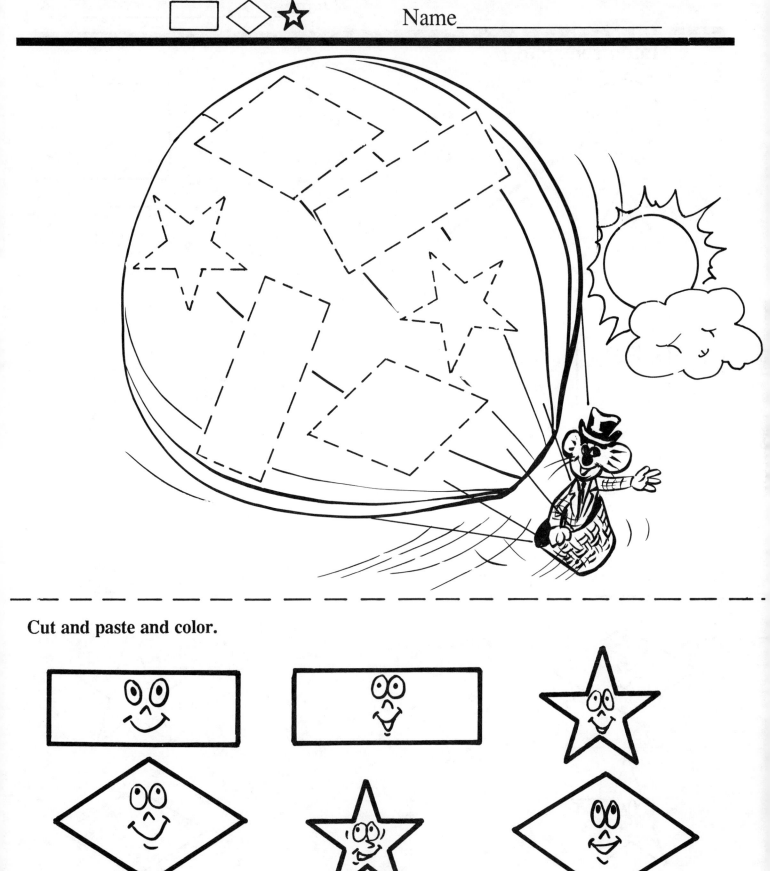

Cut and paste and color.

Name_____

Match the shapes.

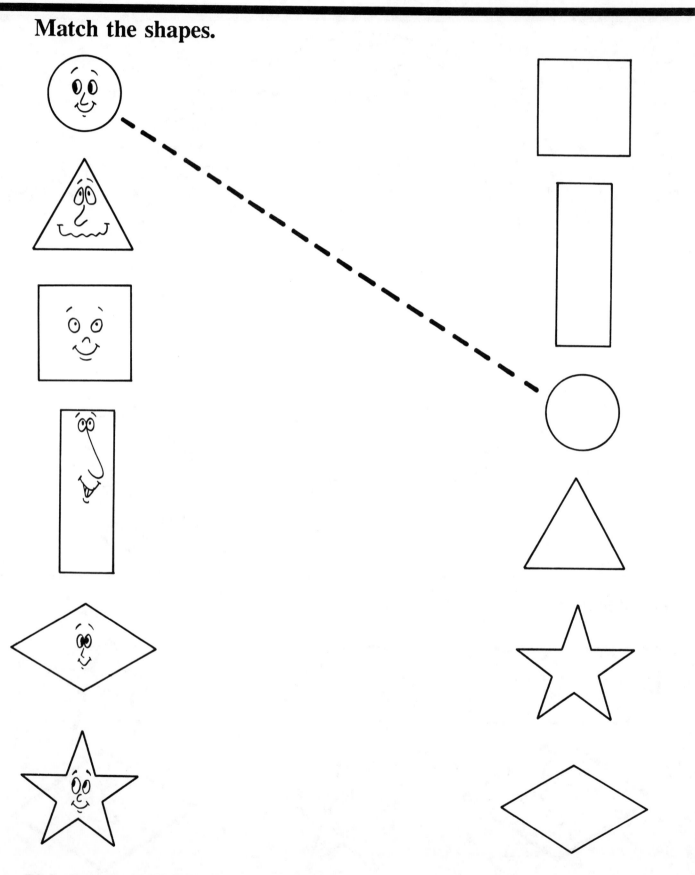

Name_____

Color the ⬡ red. Color the ▭ green.

Color the □ blue. Color the ◇ orange.

Color the △ yellow.

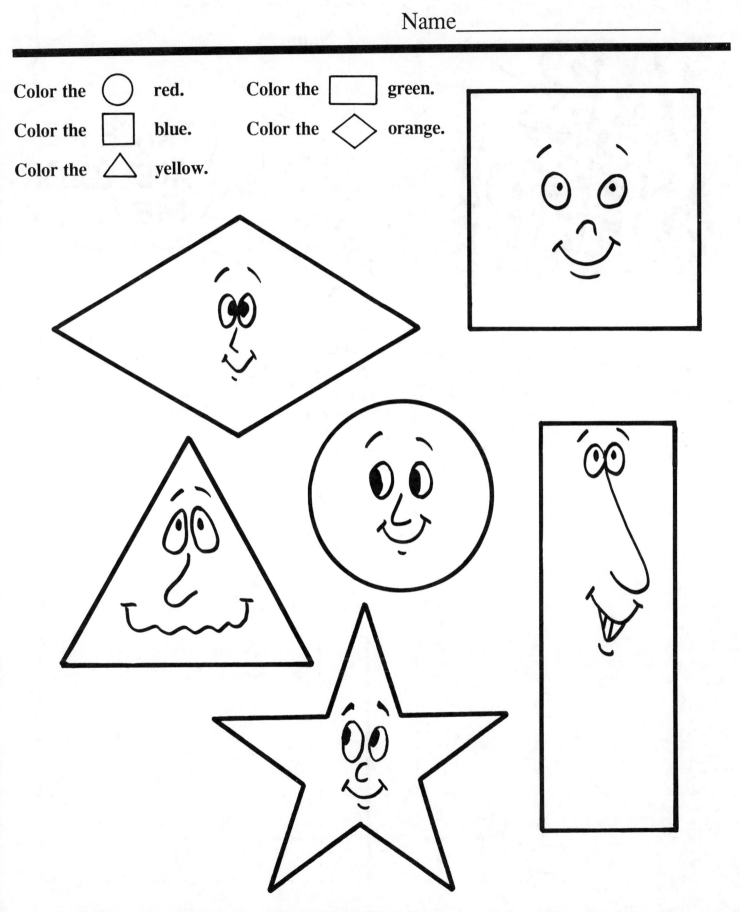

Name_____

I have learned 6 Shapes!

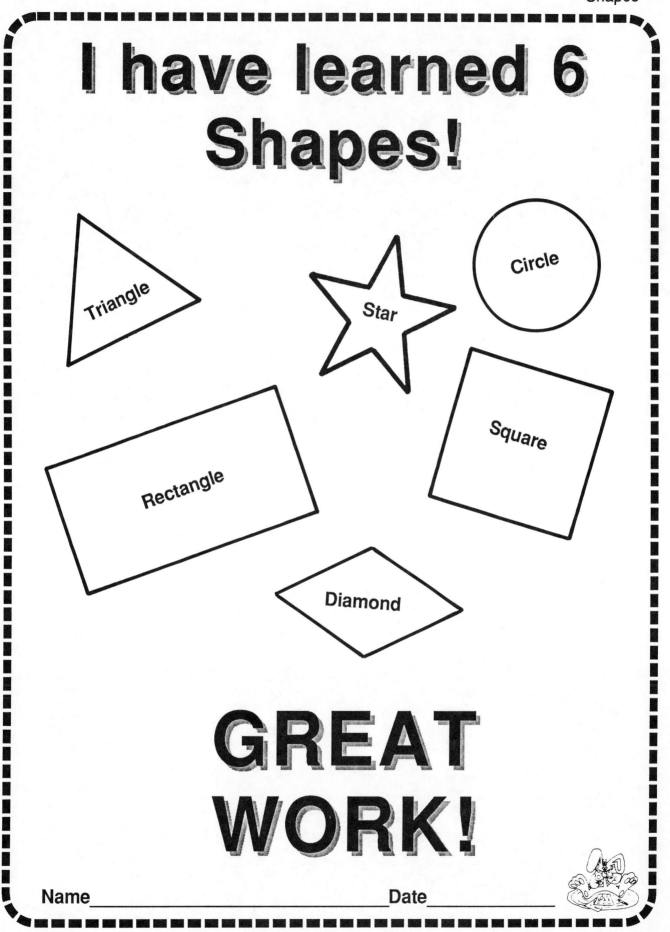

Triangle

Star

Circle

Rectangle

Square

Diamond

GREAT WORK!

Name_____Date_____

Colors

This is the color **Red**

Let's learn what the color red looks like.
Color the picture red.

Let's print the color word "red".

Red red

Can you read the color word "red"? Circle all the "red" words.

red	bed	Red	red
aed	red	Red	ret

The Apple Tree

Color the apples red.
Cut them out.
Paste the red apples
on the apple tree.

This is the color Blue

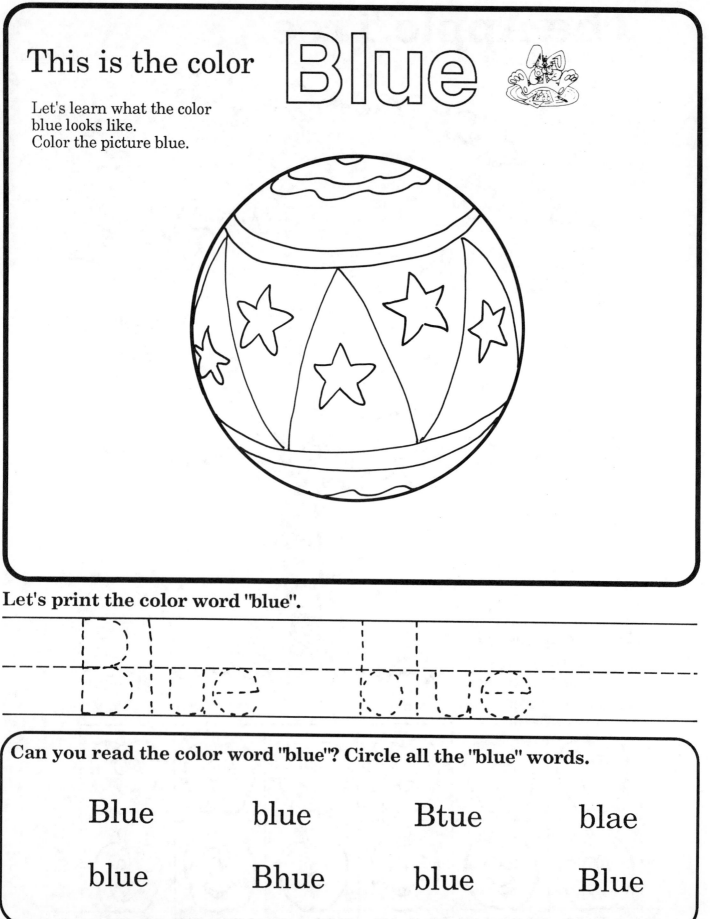

Let's learn what the color
blue looks like.
Color the picture blue.

Let's print the color word "blue".

Blue   blue

Can you read the color word "blue"? Circle all the "blue" words.

Blue	blue	Btue	blae
blue	Bhue	blue	Blue

Color the pictures. Cut them out.

Paste the red pictures under the word red.   Paste the blue pictures under the word blue.

Red   # Blue

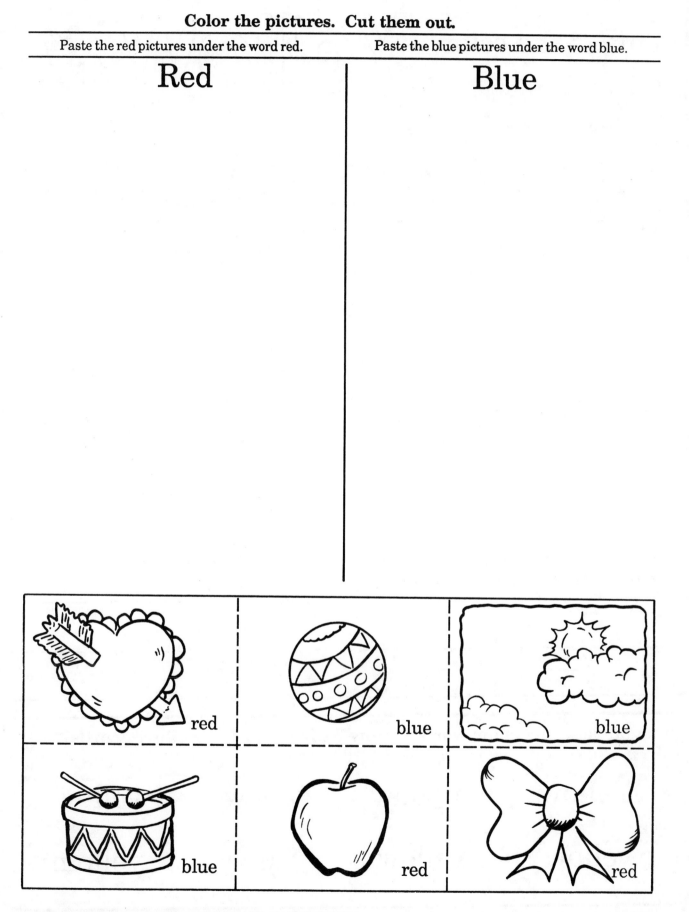

red

blue

blue

blue

red

red

This is the color Yellow

Let's learn what the color
yellow looks like.
Color the picture yellow.

Let's print the color word "yellow".

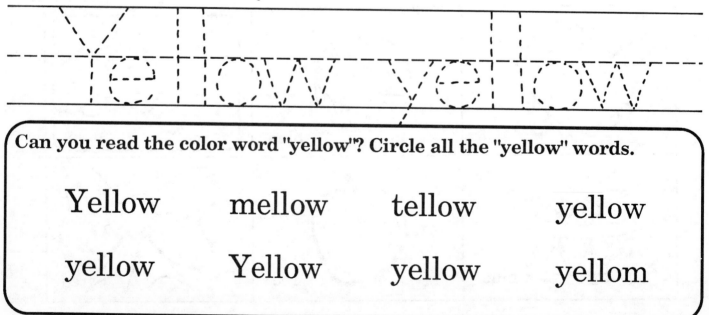

Can you read the color word "yellow"? Circle all the "yellow" words.

Yellow	mellow	tellow	yellow
yellow	Yellow	yellow	yellom

Beautiful Birds

Read the words.
Color the birds.
(Red - Blue - Yellow)

This is the color Green

Let's learn what the color green looks like.
Color the picture green.

Let's print the color word "green".

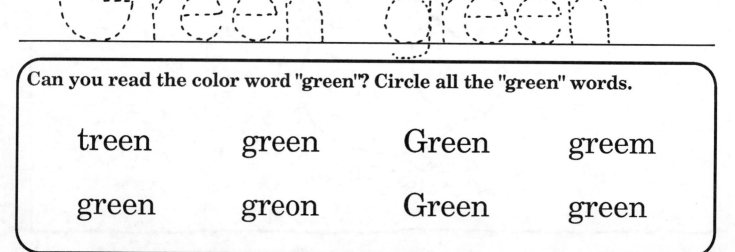

Can you read the color word "green"? Circle all the "green" words.

treen	green	Green	greem
green	greon	Green	green

Cut, paste, color.

RED

YELLOW

GREEN

BLUE

This is the color Orange

Let's learn what the color
orange looks like.
Color the picture orange.

Let's print the color word "orange".

Can you read the color word "orange"? Circle all the "orange" words.

Orange	orange	aronge	orange
orange	brange	orange	erange

Belinda the Butterfly.

Read the words.
Color Belinda the Butterfly.

green

green

blue

blue

orange

orange

red

yellow

red

yellow

red

Let's paint with colors.

Read the words.
Color the buckets and brushes.

This is the color Purple

Let's learn what the color purple looks like.
Color the picture purple.

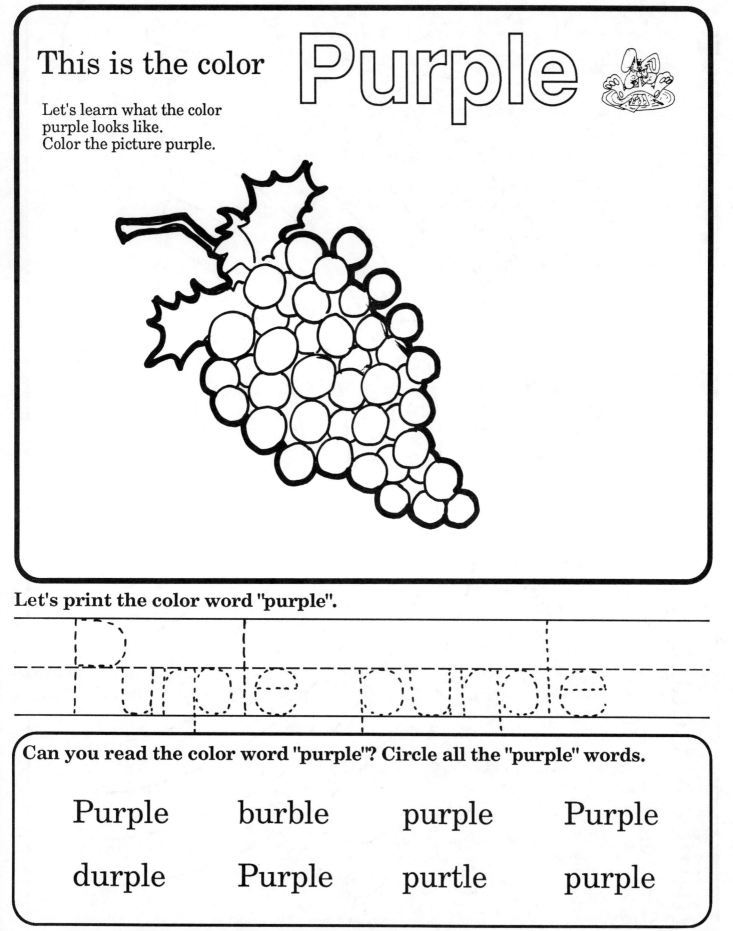

Let's print the color word "purple".

P̲u̲r̲p̲l̲e̲ ̲p̲u̲r̲p̲l̲e̲

Can you read the color word "purple"? Circle all the "purple" words.

Purple	burble	purple	Purple
durple	Purple	purtle	purple

Rainbow Colors

Color the picture.

T.S. Denison & Co., Inc./Early Childhood Basic Skills Activities

This is the color Brown

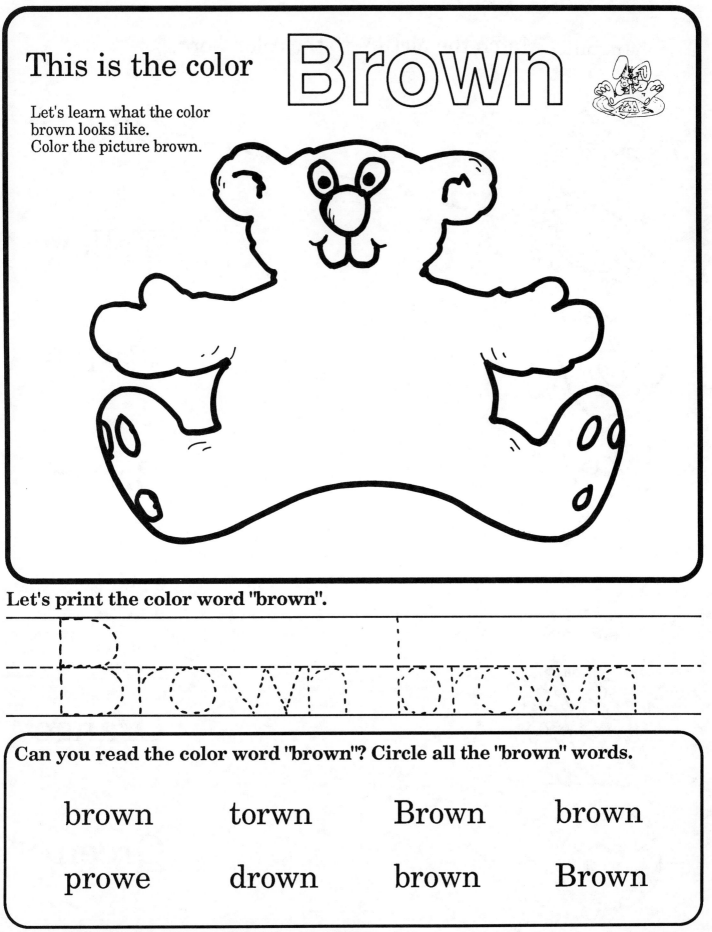

Let's learn what the color
brown looks like.
Color the picture brown.

Let's print the color word "brown".

Brown brown

Can you read the color word "brown"? Circle all the "brown" words.

brown	torwn	Brown	brown
prowe	drown	brown	Brown

Color the picture. **Match the picture to the color word.**

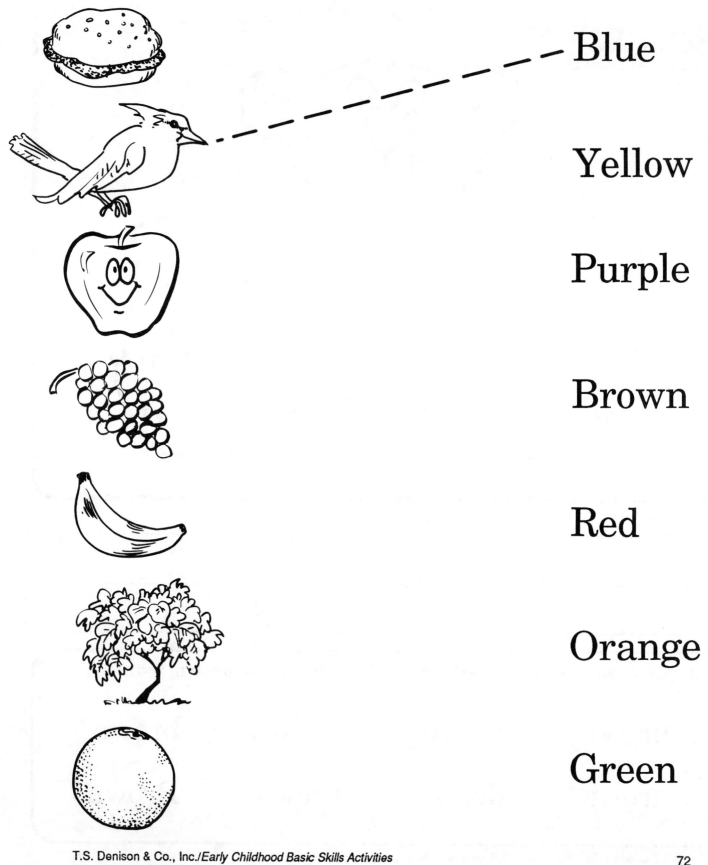

Blue

Yellow

Purple

Brown

Red

Orange

Green

This is the color Black

Let's learn what the color black looks like.
Color the picture black.

Let's print the color word "black".

Black black

Can you read the color word "black"? Circle all the "black" words.

black	Black	dlack	black
plaek	black	Black	blacp

Panda and Balloons

Color the picture.
Each number is a color.
Use the chart to color the
bear and balloons.

1 = red	5 = orange
2 = blue	6 = purple
3 = yellow	7 = brown
4 = green	8 = black

This is the color White

Let's learn what the color white looks like.
Color the picture white.

Let's print the color word "white".

White white

Can you read the color word "white"? Circle all the "white" words.

| White | mhite | white | whipe |
| white | White | whate | white |

A Hidden Picture!

Read the words. Color the picture.

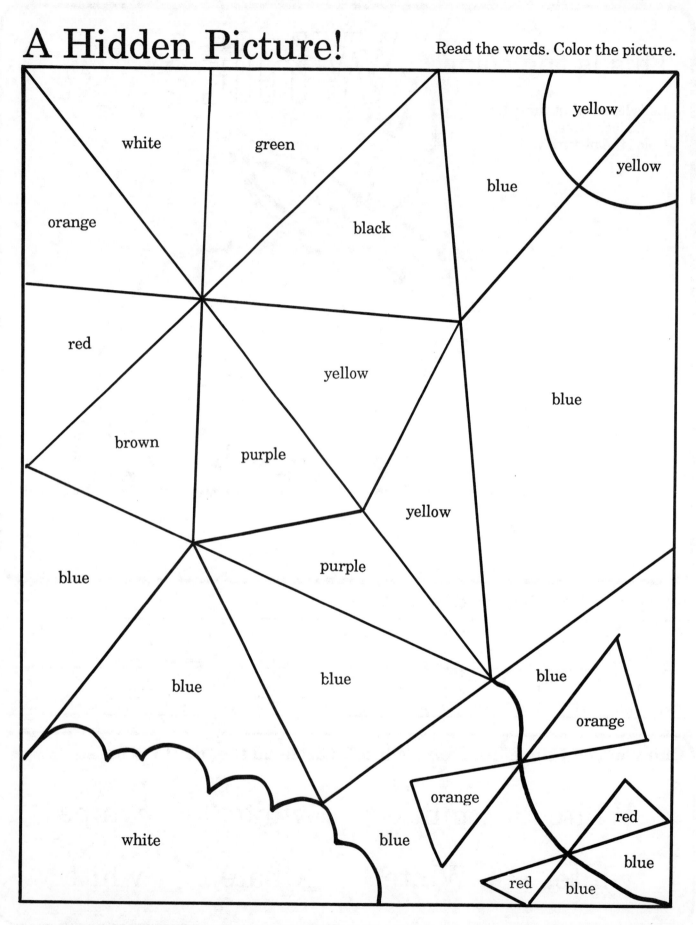

This is the color Pink

Let's learn what the color pink looks like.
Color the picture pink.

Let's print the color word "pink".

Pink   pink

Can you read the color word "pink"? Circle all the "pink" words.

Pink	wink	pink	pink
pink	Pink	link	pinh

Color the pictures.

Color the   **yellow.**

Color the   **black.**

Color the   **purple.**

Color the   **red.**

Color the   **orange.**

Color the   **white.**

Color the   **blue.**

Color the   **green .**

Color the   **brown.**

Color the   **pink.**

COLOR THE CRAYONS

Cut out and paste the color words in the sentences. Color the pictures.

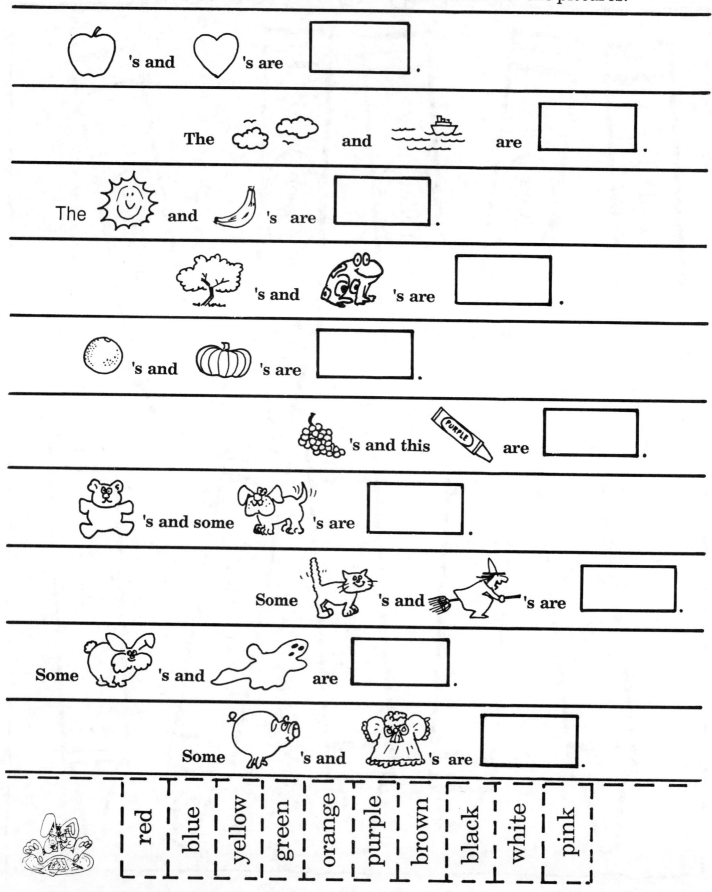

's and ❤'s are ☐.

The ☁☁ and 🚢 are ☐.

The ☀ and 🍌's are ☐.

🌳's and 🐸's are ☐.

🍊's and 🎃's are ☐.

🍇's and this PURPLE are ☐.

🧸's and some 🐕's are ☐.

Some 🐱's and 🧙's are ☐.

Some 🐶's and 👻 are ☐.

Some 🐷's and 🐘's are ☐.

red | blue | yellow | green | orange | purple | brown | black | white | pink

_____ can

name the colors
and
read and print
COLOR WORDS!

TERRIFIC!   WONDERFUL!   FABULOUS!

green   brown   blue   red   purple

pink

yellow

SUPER!

green

pink   orange   white

red

black   blue

yellow   purple

orange

Readiness
Skills
And
Concepts

Color The Pictures That Are The SAME.

Cut and Paste The Toys On The Proper Shelf.

(Go-Togethers)

Color the picture that is DIFFERENT

UP/DOWN

Cut, paste, color.

HELP THE ANIMALS GET HOME

Trace over the dots.

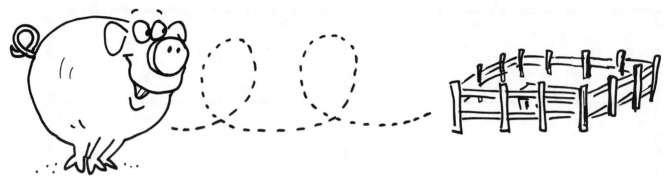

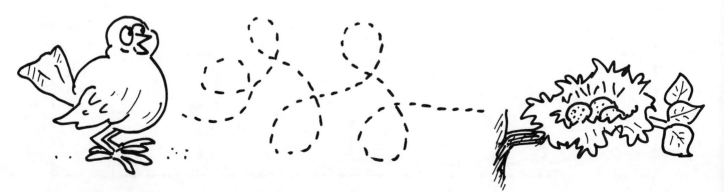

Cut and paste the BIG things on the BIG bag and the LITTLE things on the LITTLE bag.

Color the picture that comes next

(Patterning)

Which picture is next?

Cut, paste, color.

REAL/PRETEND

Color all the "real" animals.

TOP/BOTTOM   Cut, paste, color.

**Put the toys on the top shelf and the bottom shelf.
Do not put them on the middle shelf.**

SHADOWS

Draw a line from the picture to its shadow.

DAYTIME/NIGHTTIME

Cut, paste, color.

MATCH the people to the objects they use

Draw lines and color.

MATCH the animal head to its body

Cut, paste, color.

HEAR – TASTE – SMELL – FEEL

Color the things you can hear

Color the things you can taste

Color the things you can smell

Color the things you can feel

OVER/UNDER

Cut, paste, color.

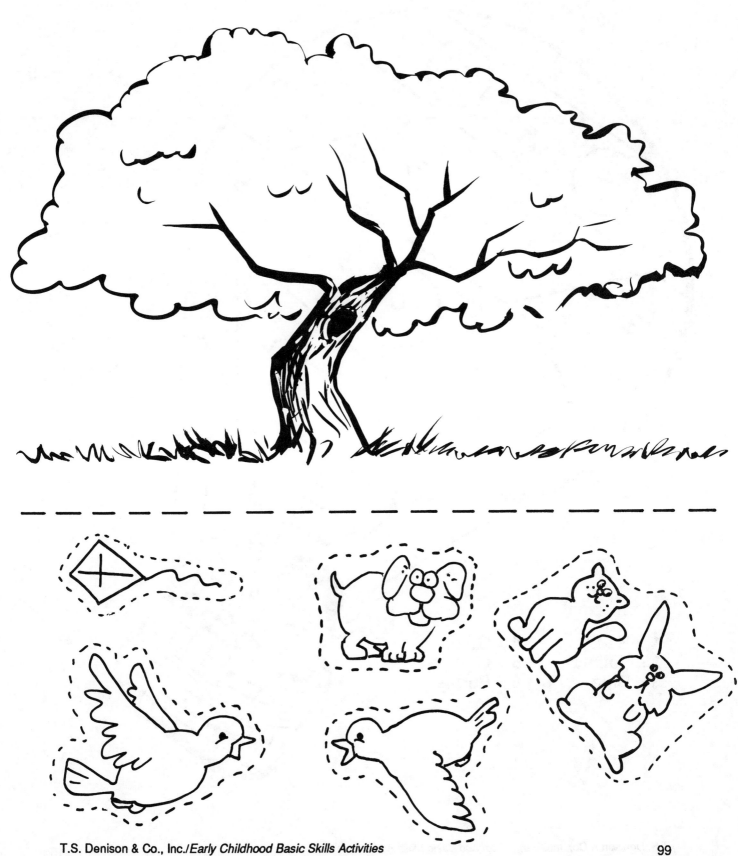

COLOR the hot-air balloon.

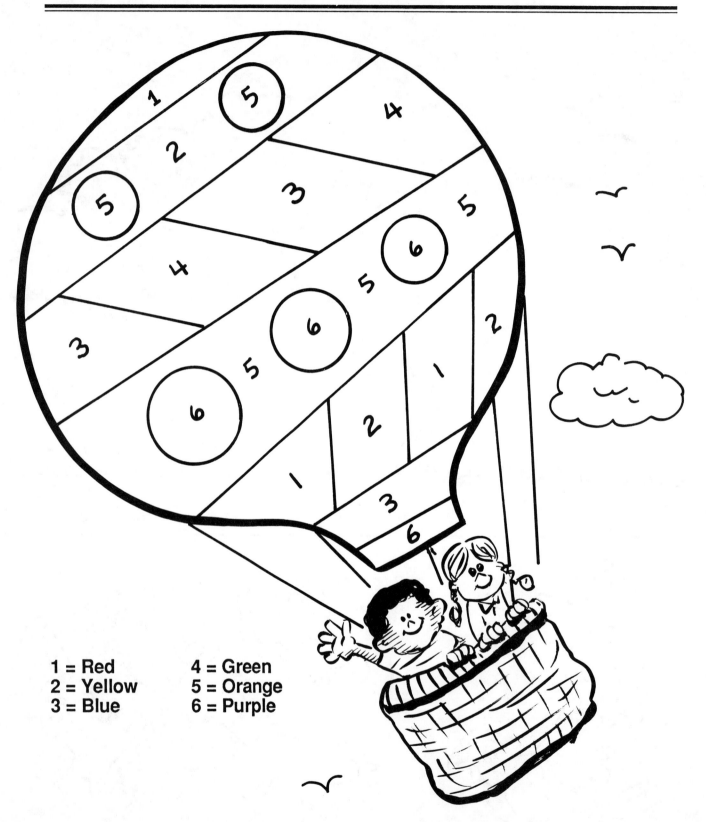

1 = Red   4 = Green
2 = Yellow 5 = Orange
3 = Blue   6 = Purple

IN/OUT

Cut, paste, color.

FOLLOW THE MAZE

Help the children find their ice cream cones.

WINTER OR SUMMER

Cut and paste the children in the correct season.

TRACE ALL THE GOOD THINGS TO EAT!

LAND – WATER – SKY

Cut, paste, and color.

TRACE AND COLOR THE SHAPES.

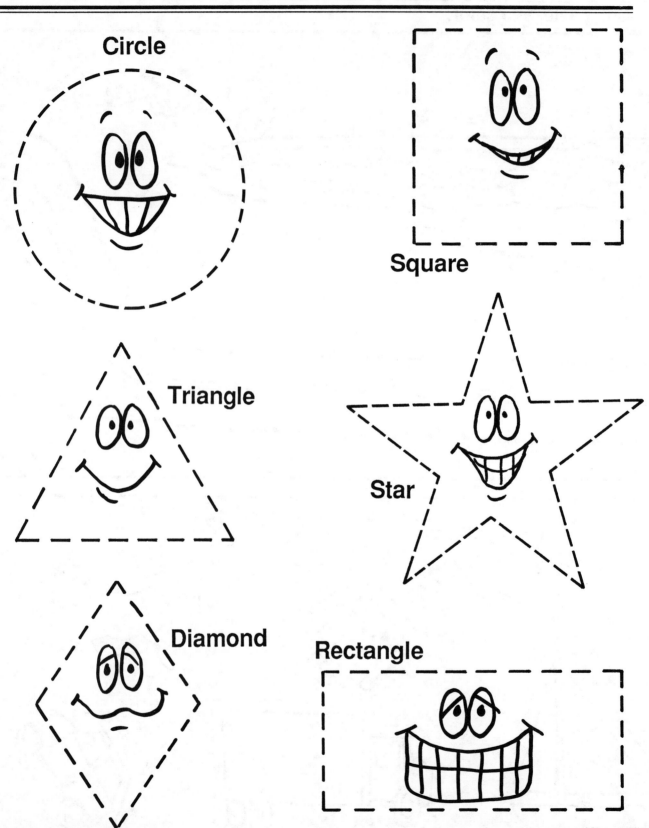

Circle

Square

Triangle

Star

Diamond

Rectangle

Child's Name   Date

has completed the Readiness Skills and Concepts Teaching Tablet

Color Your Award!

Alphabet

Letter Aa

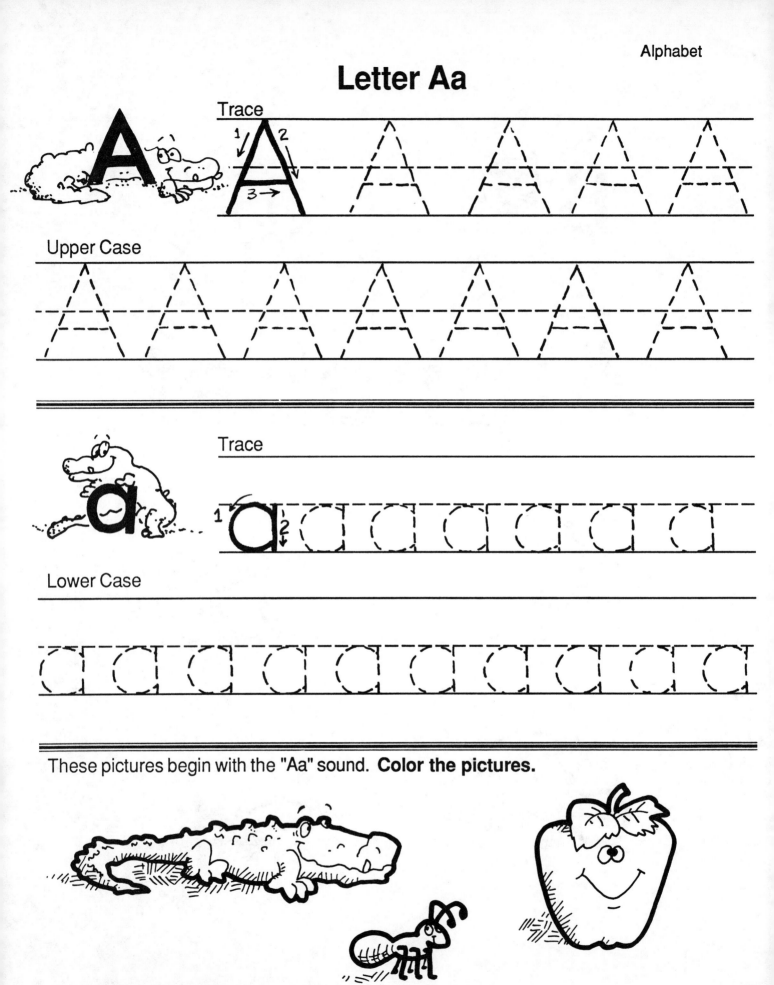

Trace

Upper Case

Trace

Lower Case

These pictures begin with the "Aa" sound. **Color the pictures.**

Letter Bb

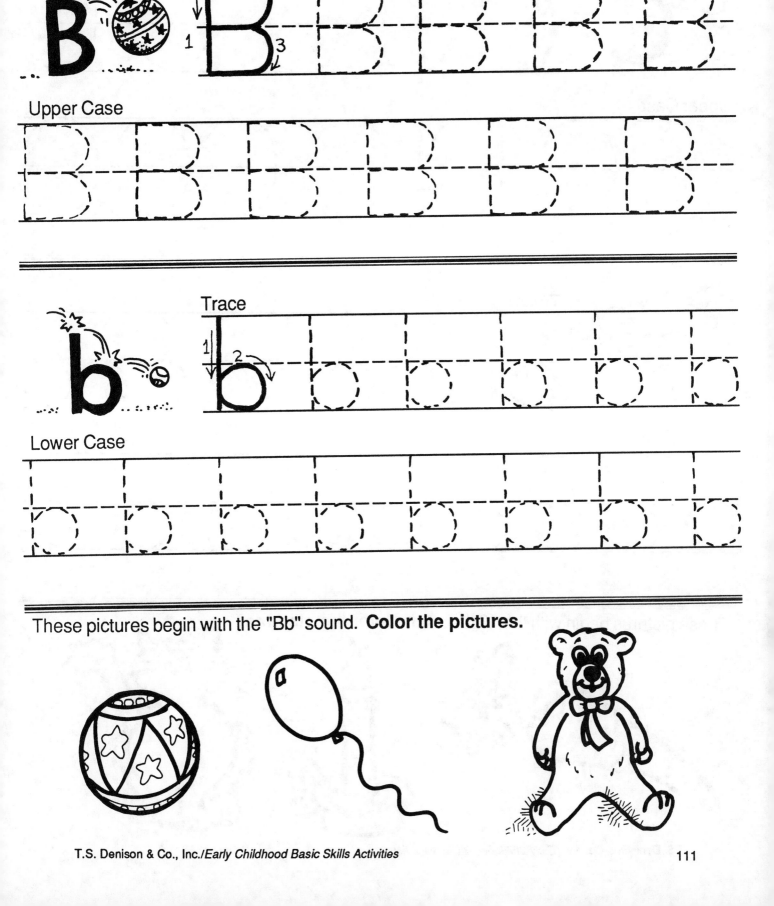

Trace

Upper Case

Trace

Lower Case

These pictures begin with the "Bb" sound. **Color the pictures.**

Letter Cc

Trace

C C C C C C

Upper Case

Trace

c c c c c c c c c

Lower Case

These pictures begin with the "Cc" sound. **Color the pictures.**

Letter Dd

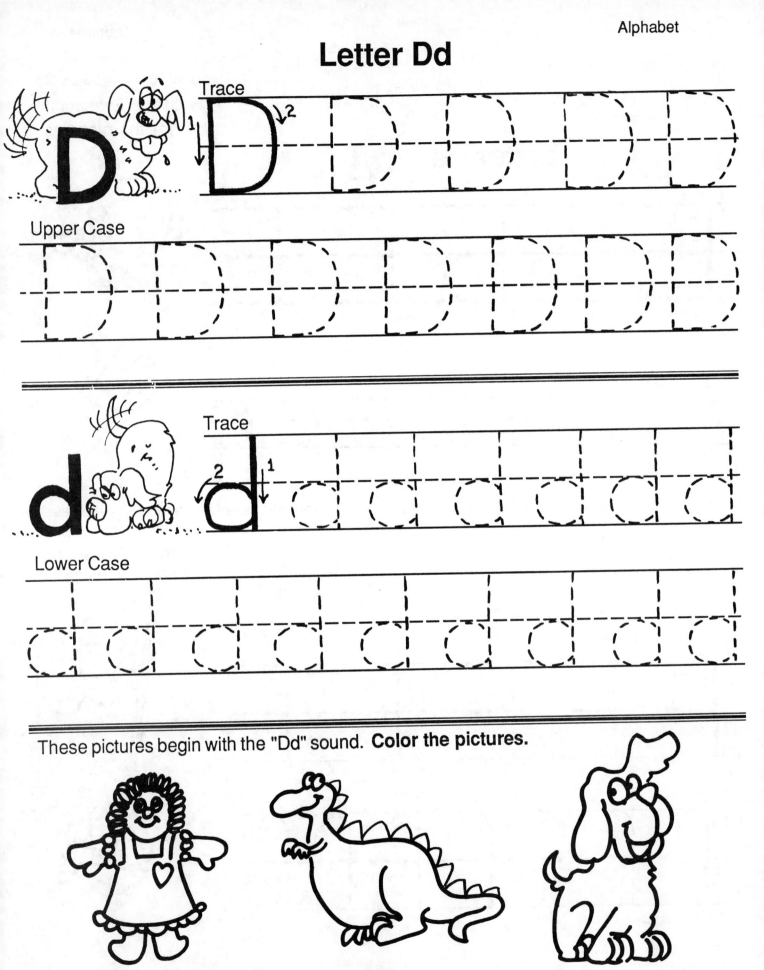

Trace

Upper Case

Trace

Lower Case

These pictures begin with the "Dd" sound. **Color the pictures.**

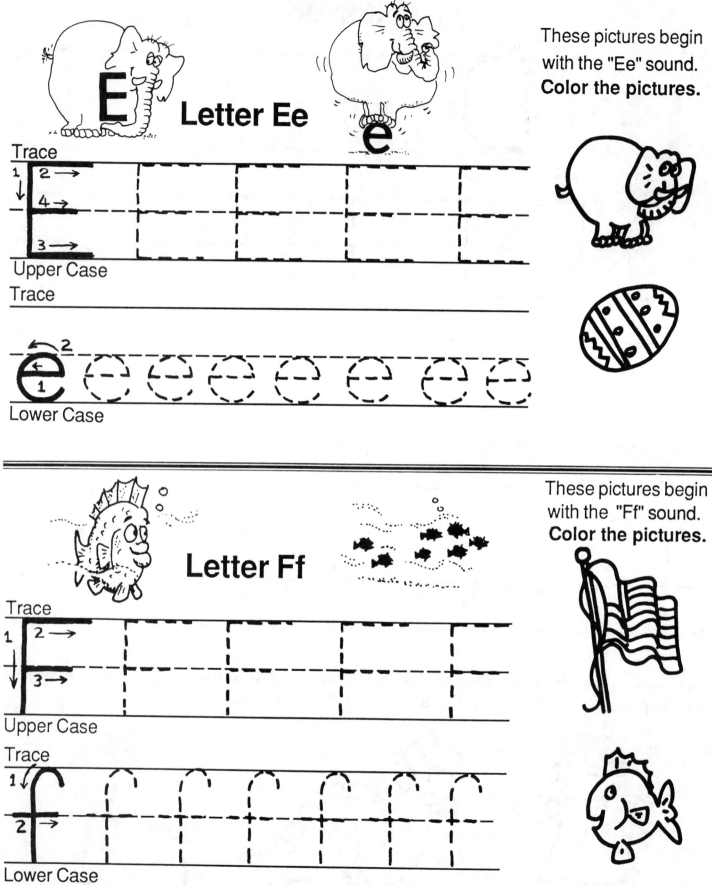

Letter Ee

These pictures begin with the "Ee" sound. **Color the pictures.**

Trace

Upper Case

Trace

Lower Case

Letter Ff

These pictures begin with the "Ff" sound. **Color the pictures.**

Trace

Upper Case

Trace

Lower Case

Letter Gg

Trace

Upper Case

Trace

Lower Case

These pictures begin with the "Gg" sound. **Color the pictures.**

Letter Hh

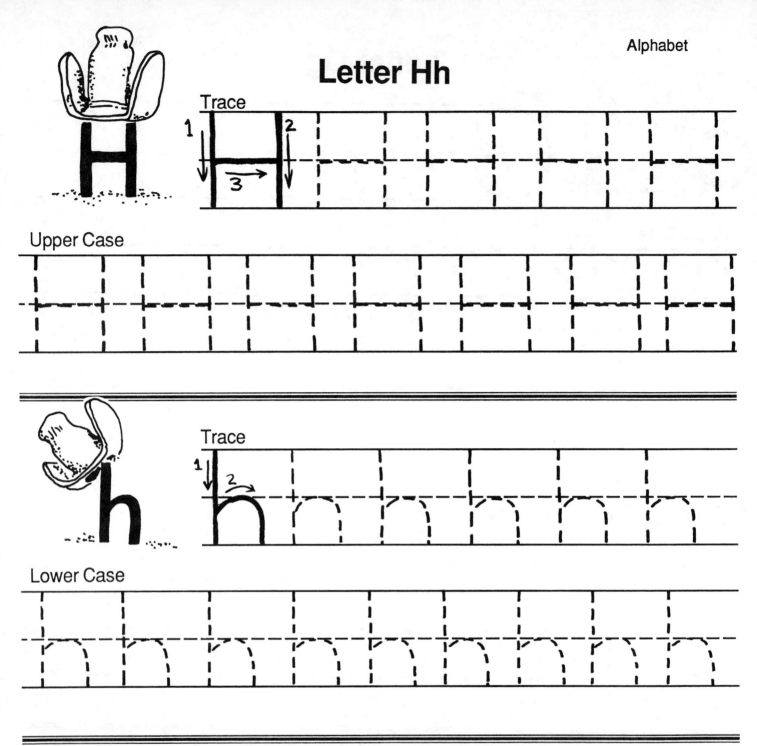

Trace

Upper Case

Trace

Lower Case

These pictures begin with the "Hh" sound. **Color the pictures.**

Letter Ii

These pictures begin with the "Ii" sound. **Color the pictures.**

Trace

Upper Case

Trace

Lower Case

Letter Jj

These pictures begin with the "Jj" sound.

Trace

Upper Case

Trace

Lower Case

Color the pictures.

Letter Kk

Trace

Upper Case

Trace

Lower Case

These pictures begin with the "Kk" sound. **Color the pictures.**

Letter Ll

Trace

1 ↓
2 →

Upper Case

Trace

1 ↓

Lower Case

These pictures begin with the "Ll" sound. **Color the pictures.**

Letter Mm

Trace

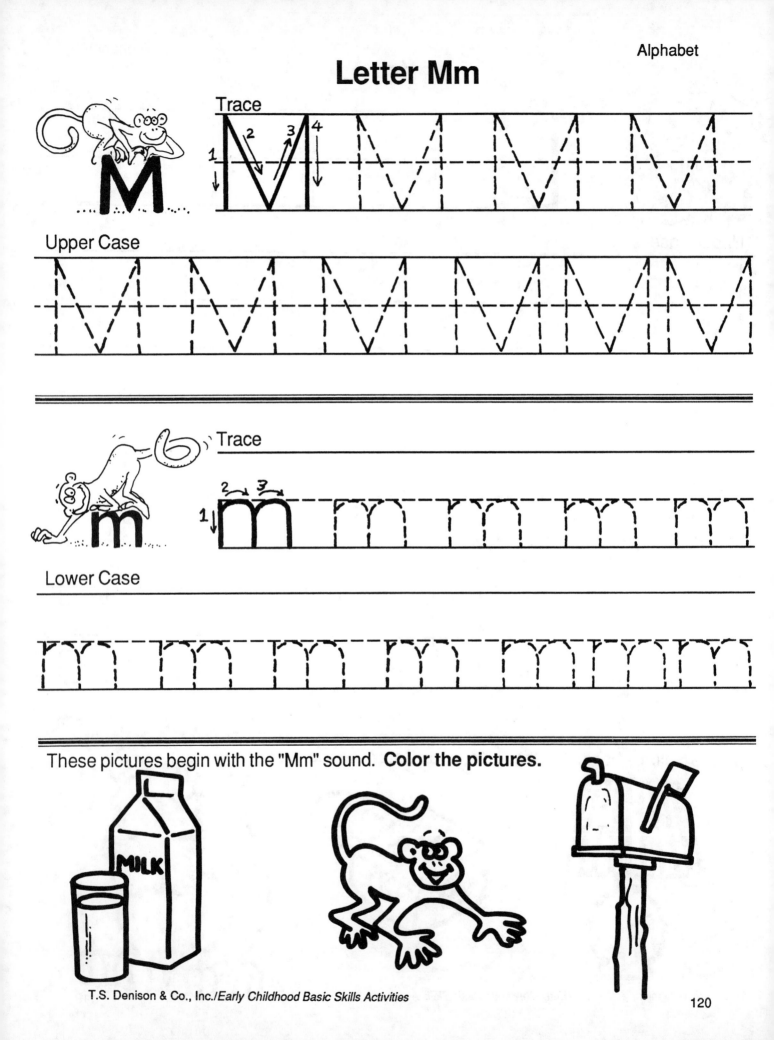

Upper Case

Trace

Lower Case

These pictures begin with the "Mm" sound. **Color the pictures.**

Letter Nn

Trace

Upper Case

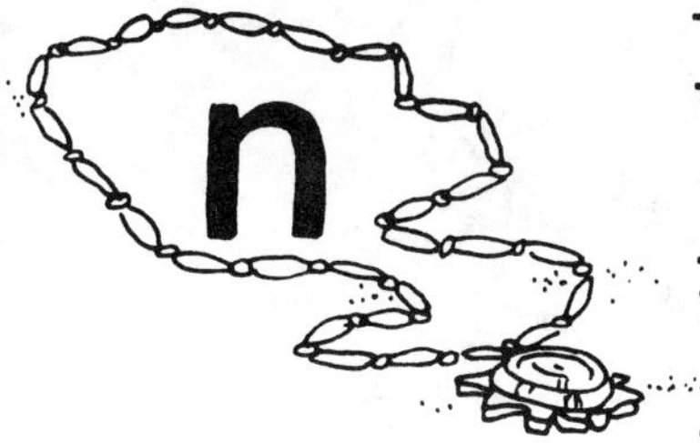

Trace

Lower Case

These pictures begin with the "Nn" sound. **Color the pictures.**

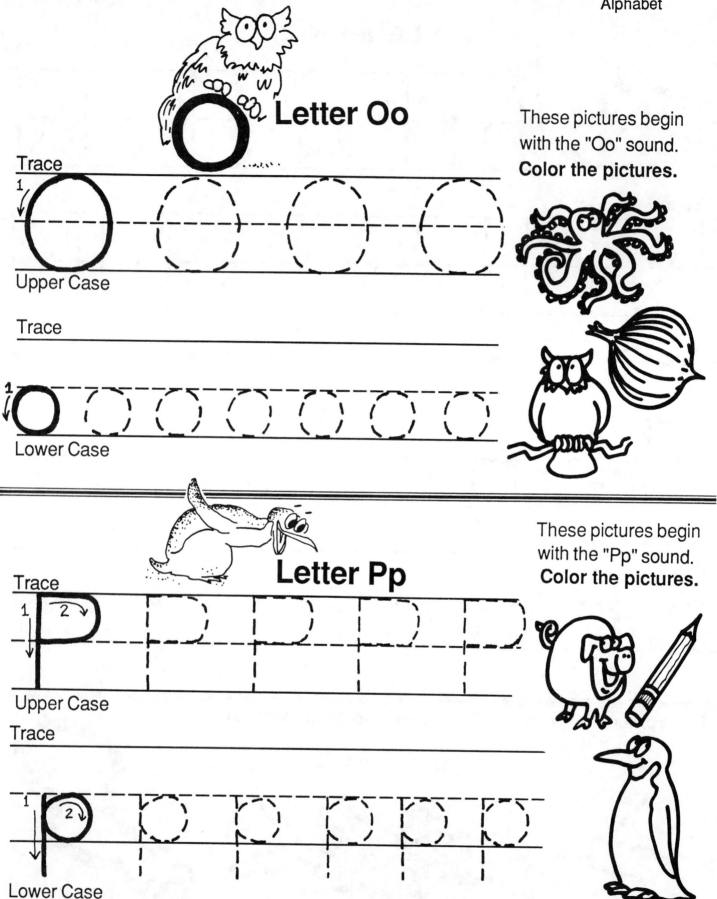

Letter Oo

These pictures begin with the "Oo" sound. **Color the pictures.**

Trace

1 ↓

Upper Case

Trace

1 ↓

Lower Case

Letter Pp

These pictures begin with the "Pp" sound. **Color the pictures.**

Trace

1 ↓ 2 ↘

Upper Case

Trace

1 ↓ 2 ↘

Lower Case

Letter Qq

Trace

Upper Case

Trace

Lower Case

These pictures begin with the "Qq" sound. **Color the pictures.**

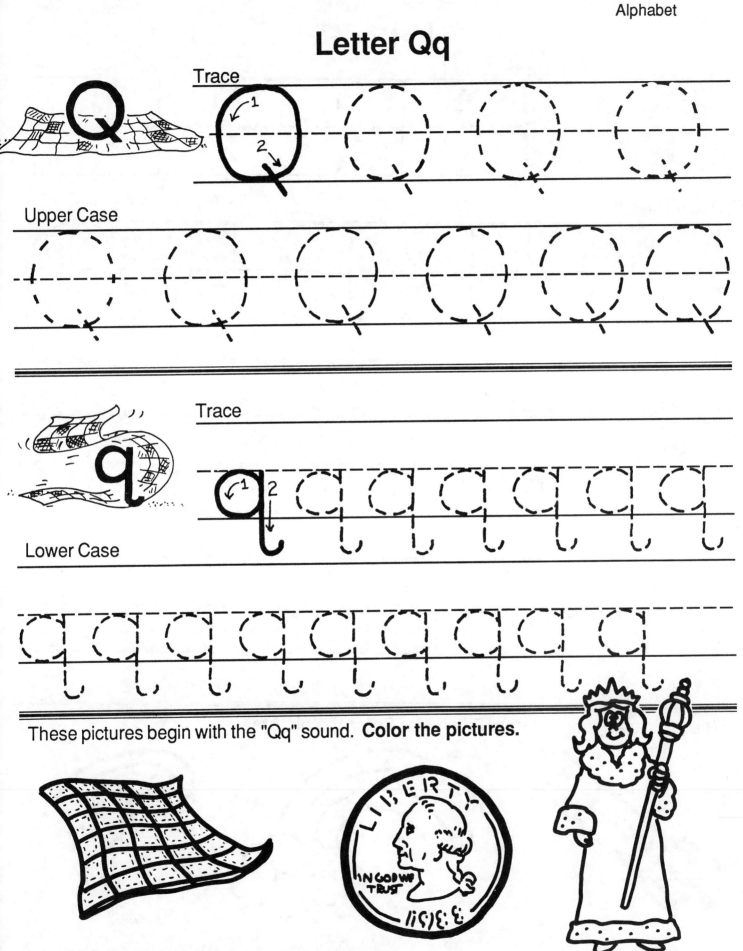

Letter Rr

Trace

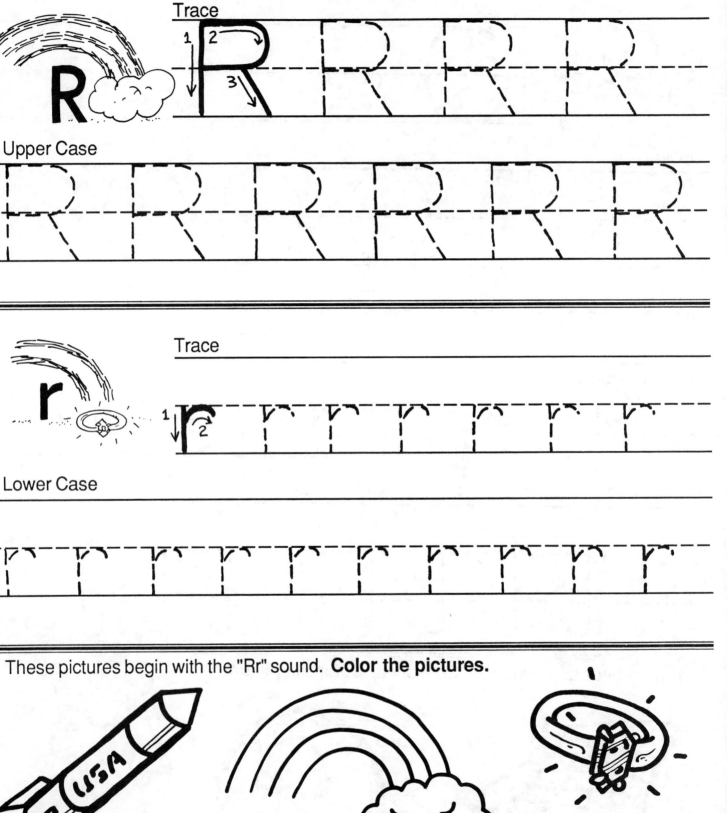

Upper Case

Trace

Lower Case

These pictures begin with the "Rr" sound. **Color the pictures.**

Letter Ss

Trace

S S S S S S S S S

Upper Case

S S S S S S S S S S

Trace

S S S S S S S S S

Lower Case

s s s s s s s s s s

These pictures begin with the "Ss" sound. **Color the pictures.**

Letter Tt

Trace

Upper Case

Trace

Lower Case

These pictures begin with the "Tt" sound. **Color the pictures.**

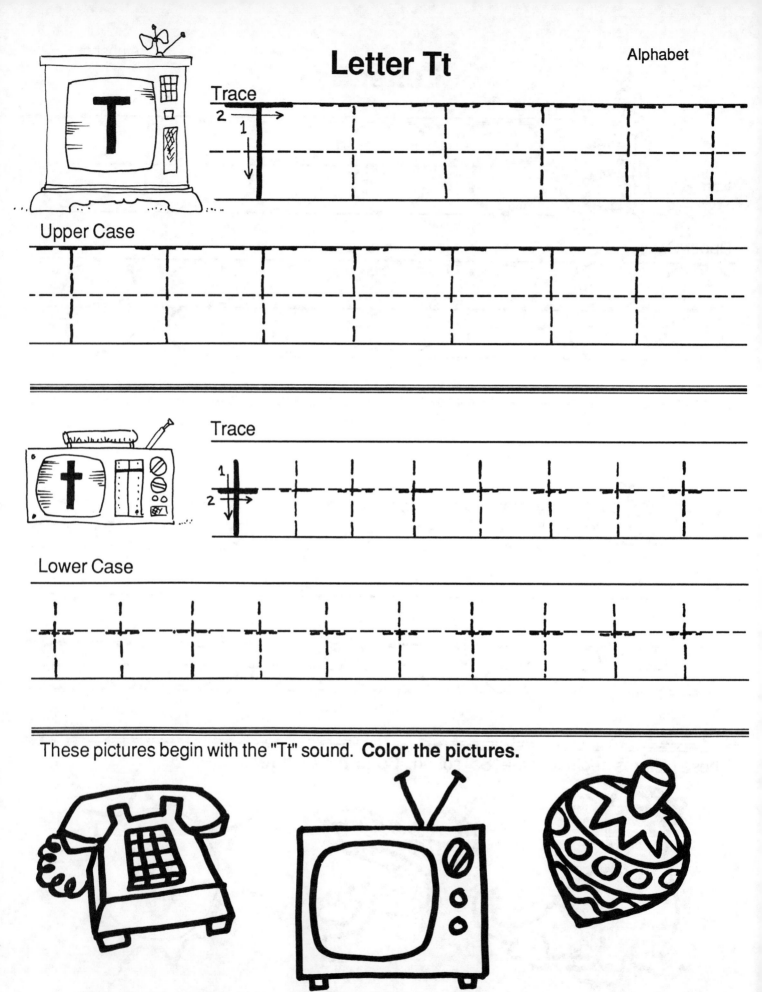

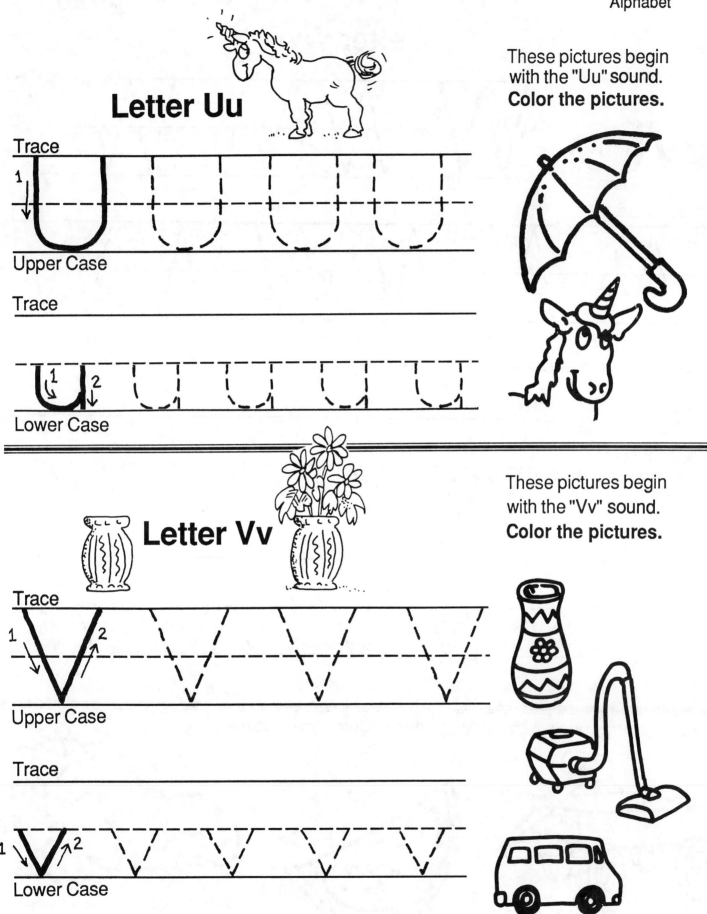

Letter Uu

Trace

1

Upper Case

Trace

1 2

Lower Case

These pictures begin with the "Uu" sound. **Color the pictures.**

Letter Vv

Trace

1 2

Upper Case

Trace

1 2

Lower Case

These pictures begin with the "Vv" sound. **Color the pictures.**

Letter Ww

Trace

Upper Case

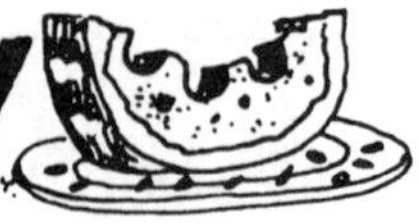

Trace

Lower Case

These pictures begin with the "Ww" sound. **Color the pictures.**

Letter Xx

These pictures begin with the "Xx" sound. **Color the pictures.**

Trace Upper Case

Trace Lower Case

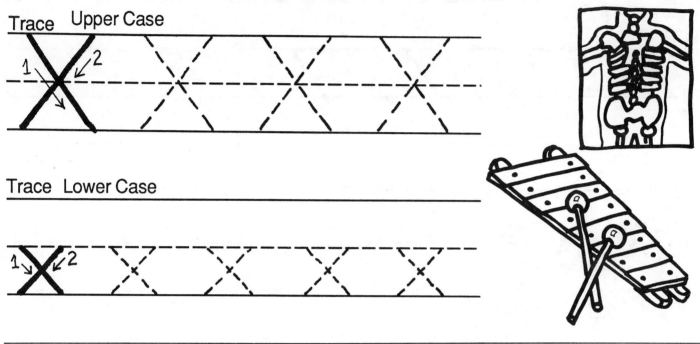

Letter Yy

These pictures begin with the "Yy" sound. **Color the pictures.**

Trace Upper Case

Trace Lower Case

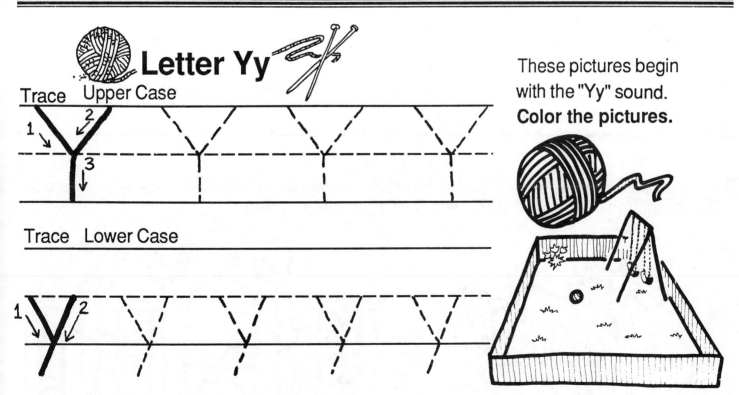

Letter Zz

Trace

Upper Case

Trace

Lower Case

These pictures begin with the "Zz" sound. **Color the pictures.**

ZOO

UPPER CASE ALPHABET

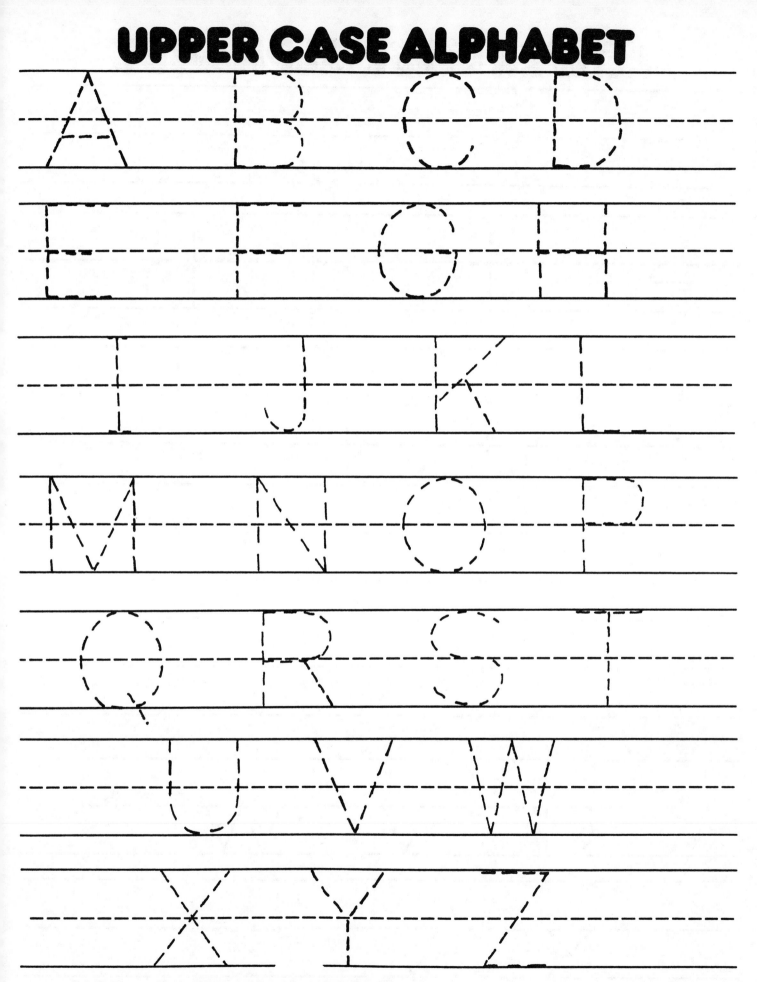

LOWER CASE ALPHABET

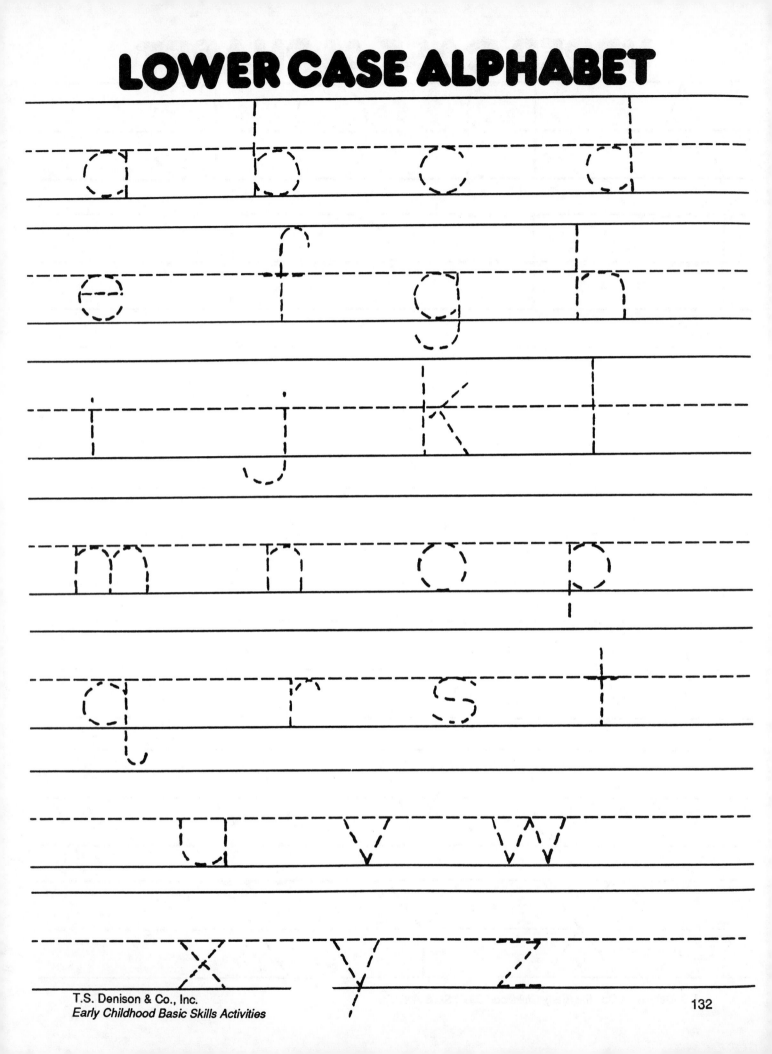

☆ THE ALPHABET AWARD ☆

I can print alphabet letters!

GREAT JOB!

Well Done!

Show off your printing-
Trace the letters
and color the picture.

Name_____

Age_____

Numbers

This is the number 1
Color the picture.

How many things are in this picture?

Let's learn how to print the number 1.

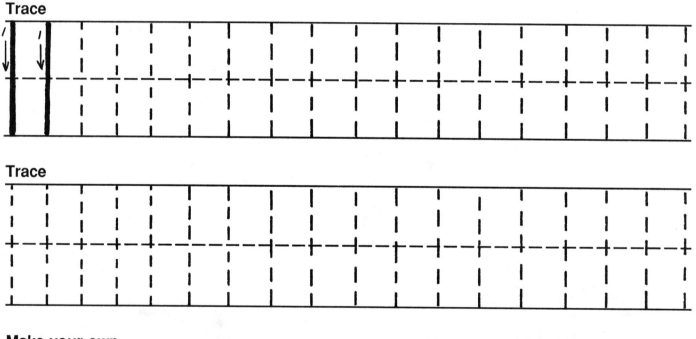

Trace

Trace

Make your own.

This is the number 2
Color the picture.

How many things are in this picture?

Let's learn how to print the number 2.

Trace

Trace

Make your own.

How Many?

Trace the correct number for each box. Color all the pictures.

This is the number 3
Color the picture.

How many things are in this picture? ☐

Let's learn how to print the number 3.

Trace

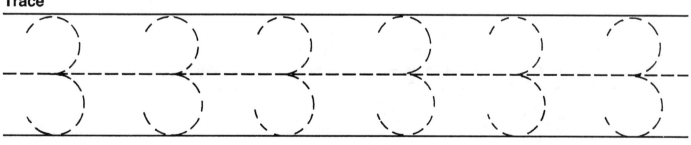

Trace

Make your own.

I Can Print and Count 1 – 2 – 3!

Trace   **Color the correct number of objects**

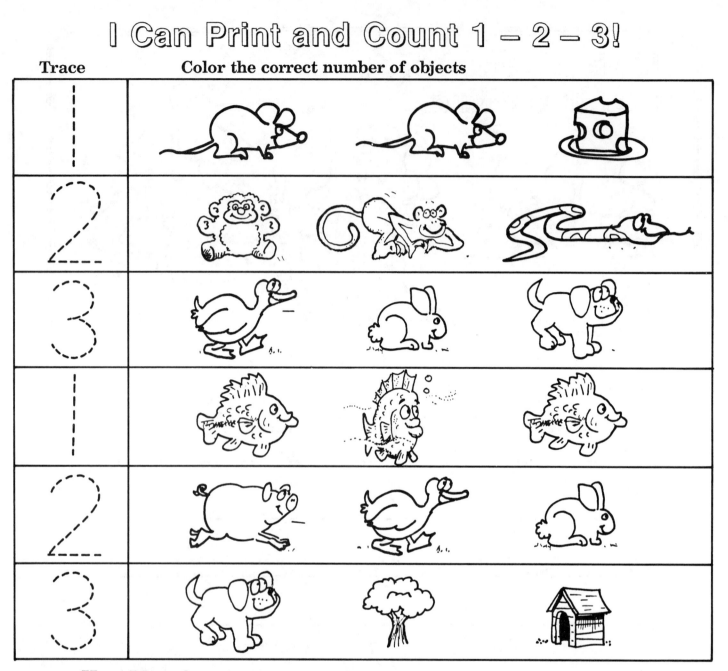

How Many? Circle the correct number in each box. Color the pictures.

This is the number 4
Color the picture.

How many things are in this picture?

Let's learn how to print the number 4.

Trace

Trace

Make your own.

Match the Numbers to the Set of Objects

Trace the numbers. Color the pictures.

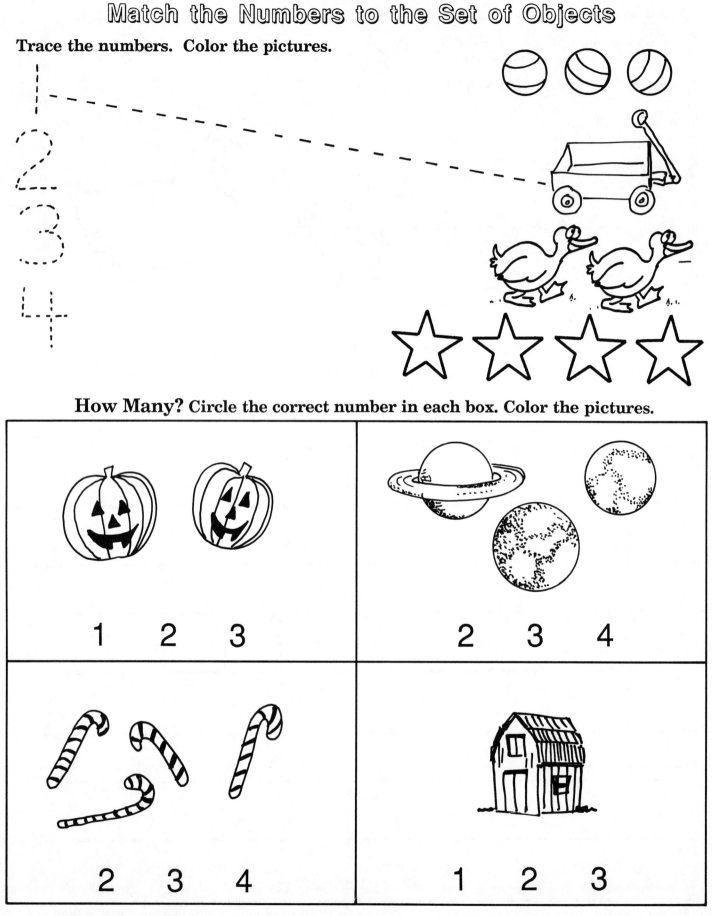

How Many? Circle the correct number in each box. Color the pictures.

This is the number 5
Color the picture.

How many things are in this picture?

Let's learn how to print the number 5.

Trace

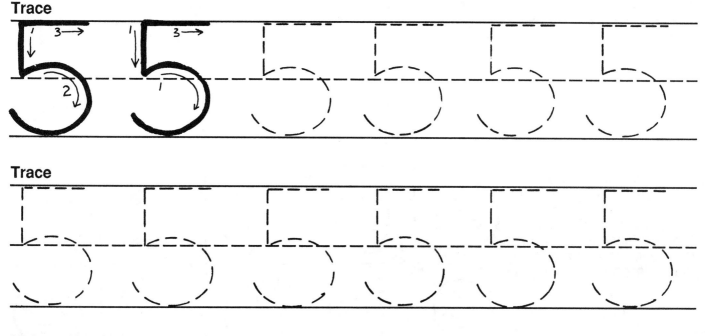

Trace

Make your own.

Cut and Paste

Trace the numbers

1	
2	
3	
4	
5	

Color the 'happy faces.'
Cut them all out.
Paste the correct number
of "happy faces" in each
box. For example next to
the 3 you should paste 3
happy faces.

How Many?

1 2 3

2 3 4

3 4 5

1 2 3

2 3 4

3 4 5

1 2 3

3 4 5

3 4 5

1 2 3

Circle the correct number. Color the pictures.

Take a Good Look at the Zoo!

How Many?
Can you count all the animals
at the zoo?
Write the correct number next
to each box.

Color all the animals

This is the number 6
Color the picture.

How many things are in this picture?

Let's learn how to print the number 6

Trace

6 6 6 6 6

Trace

6 6 6 6 6

Make your own.

Finish Each Picture

Draw **1** balloon for the boy.

Draw **2** scoops of ice cream on the cone.

Draw **3** fish in the fish bowl.

Draw **4** legs on the horse.

Draw **5** apples on the tree.

Draw **6** cookies on the plate.

This is the number 7
Color the picture.

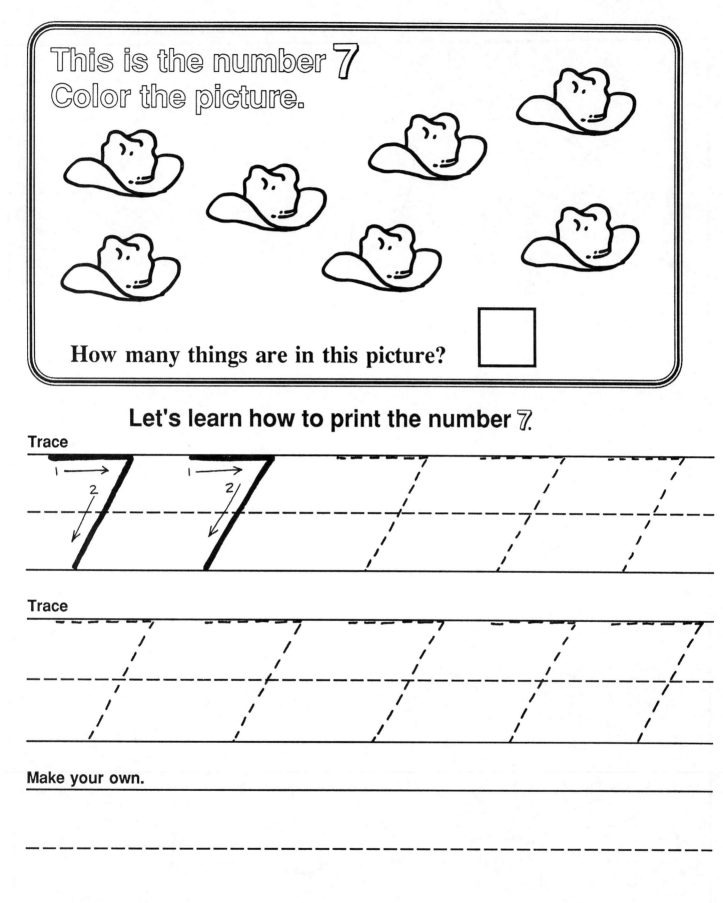

How many things are in this picture?

Let's learn how to print the number 7.

Trace

Trace

Make your own.

Trace the numbers. Draw balloons on the strings. Count and color them.

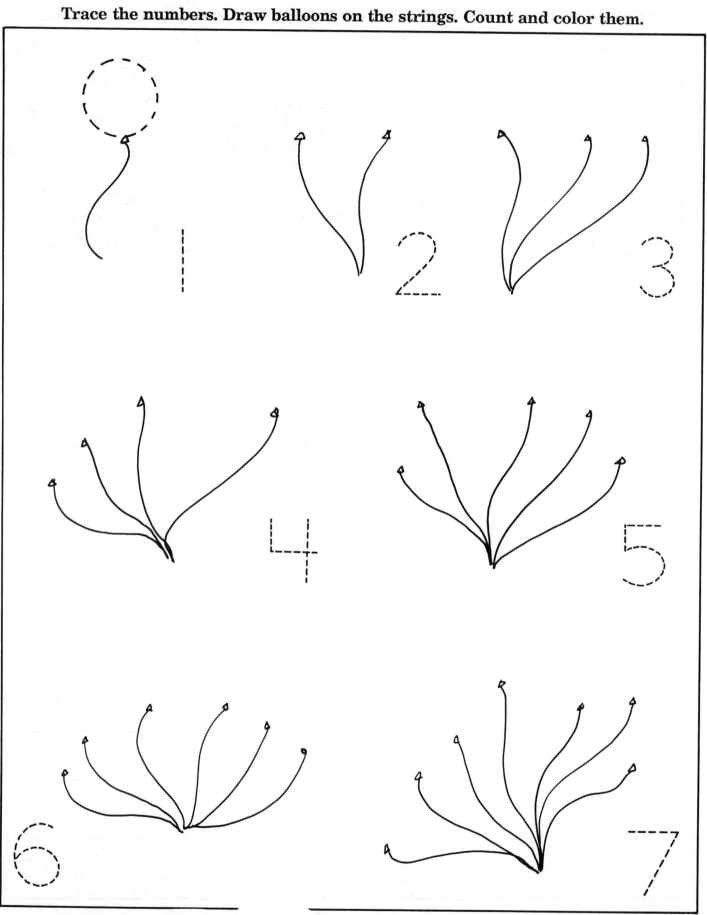

This is the number 8
Color the picture.

How many things are in this picture?

Let's learn how to print the number 8

Trace

Trace

Make your own.

Numbers 1 through 8

Trace the number. Color the correct number of objects in each box.

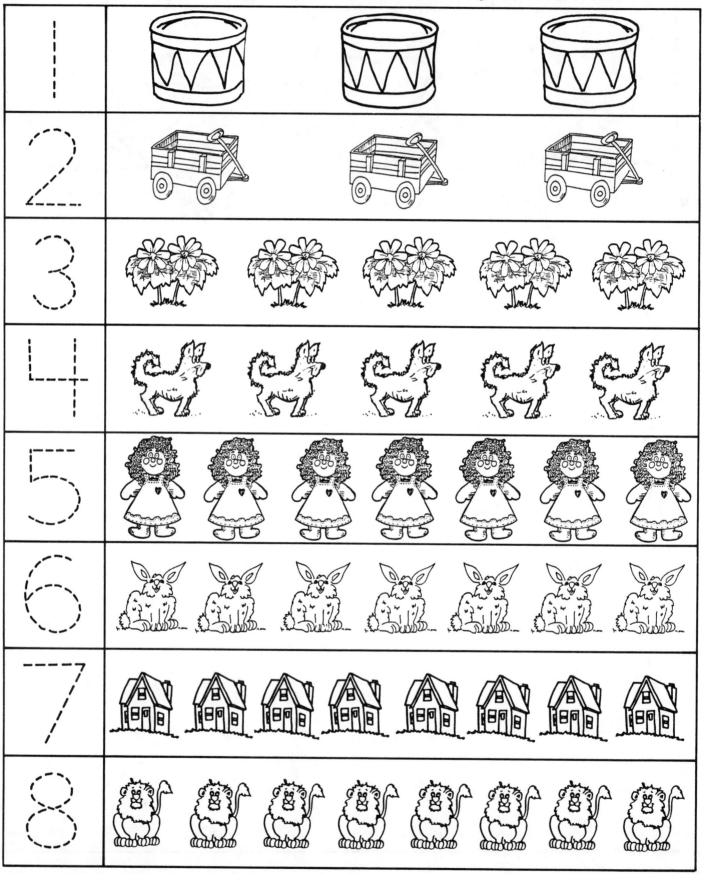

This is the number 9
Color the picture.

How many things are in this picture?

Let's learn how to print the number 9.

Trace

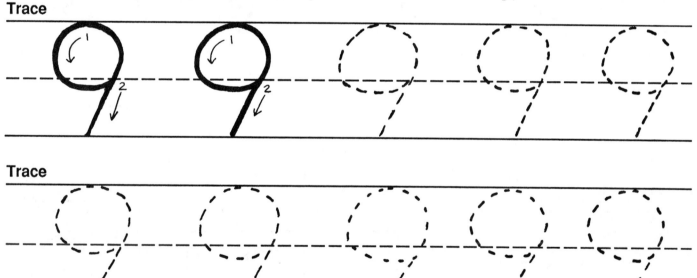

Trace

Make your own.

How Many? – Numbers 1 through 9

CUT AND PASTE

1 2 3 4
5 6 7 8 9

Count the objects in each box. Cut out the numbers.
Paste the correct number in each box.
Color all the pictures.

This is the number 10
Color the picture.

How many things are in this picture?

Let's learn how to print the number 10

Trace

Trace

Make your own.

How Many?

Circle the correct number for each box.

1 2 3

4 5 6

7 8 9

2 3 4

5 6 7

8 9 10

3 4 5

6 7 8

4 5 6

8 9 10

Counting 1 to 10

How Many?

Write the correct number next to each box.

Color the picture.

Trace the number. Color the correct amount of objects in each box.

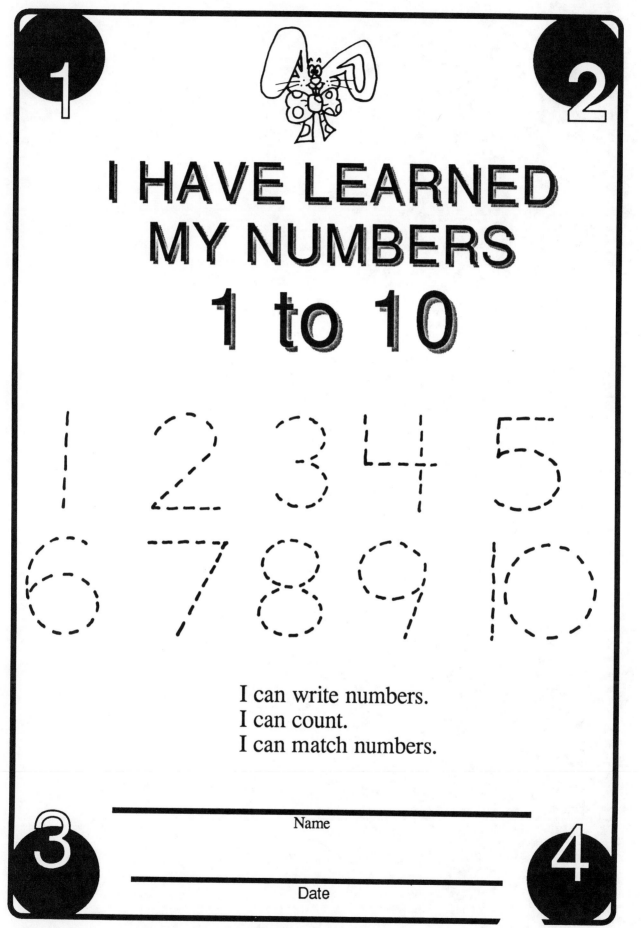

I HAVE LEARNED
MY NUMBERS
1 to 10

I can write numbers.
I can count.
I can match numbers.

_____
Name

_____
Date

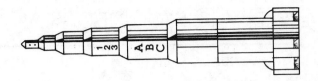

Cut, Color and Paste Puzzles

BARRY BRONTOSAURUS

**This is a large puzzle.
You will find all the pieces
on pages 162 and 163.
Color the pieces.
Cut them out.
Put them together.**

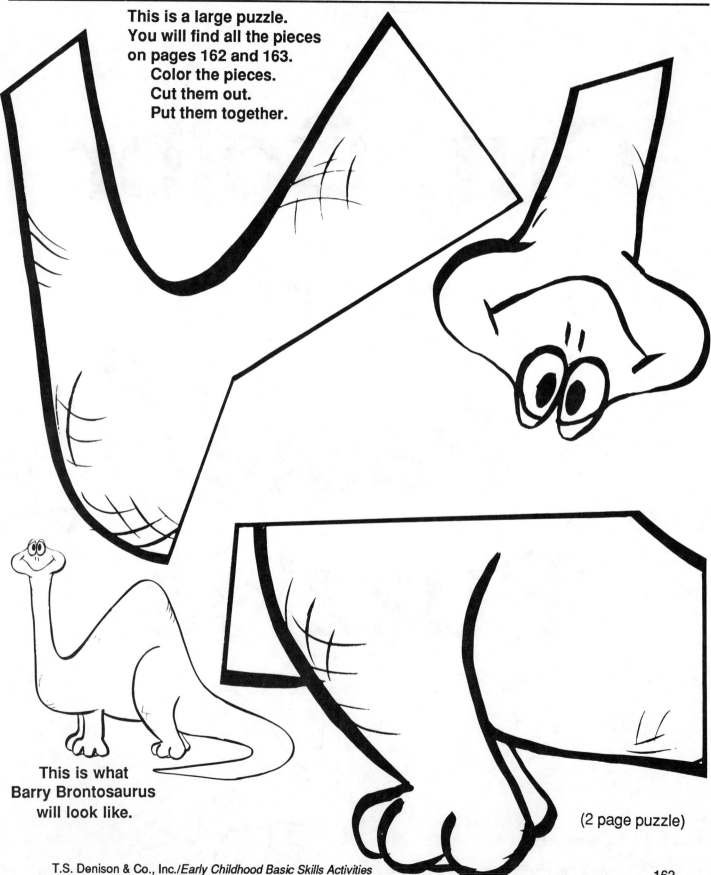

**This is what
Barry Brontosaurus
will look like.**

(2 page puzzle)

Keep the pieces in an envelope and you can use the puzzle over and over again. **OR:** you can paste the puzzle pieces on a large sheet of paper (11x17) or on a grocery bag.

FOREST FRIENDS

Color the picture. Cut along the dotted lines. Have fun playing with the puzzle.

PADDY PANDA PUZZLE

Cut out the pieces. Paste them on the Panda puzzle shape.

UNICORN

Puzzle pieces on page 167

Unicorn Puzzle Pieces

Cut out the unicorn puzzle pieces.
Put the pieces together on the
unicorn shape found on page166.

Color the pieces.

Save the puzzle pieces to use again,
OR: paste them on the unicorn shape.

SUPER DUPER ICE CREAM CONE

Color the pieces of the ice cream cone.
Cut them out.
Paste them on a piece of paper.
You will have a *super duper ice cream cone.*

TEDDY BEAR

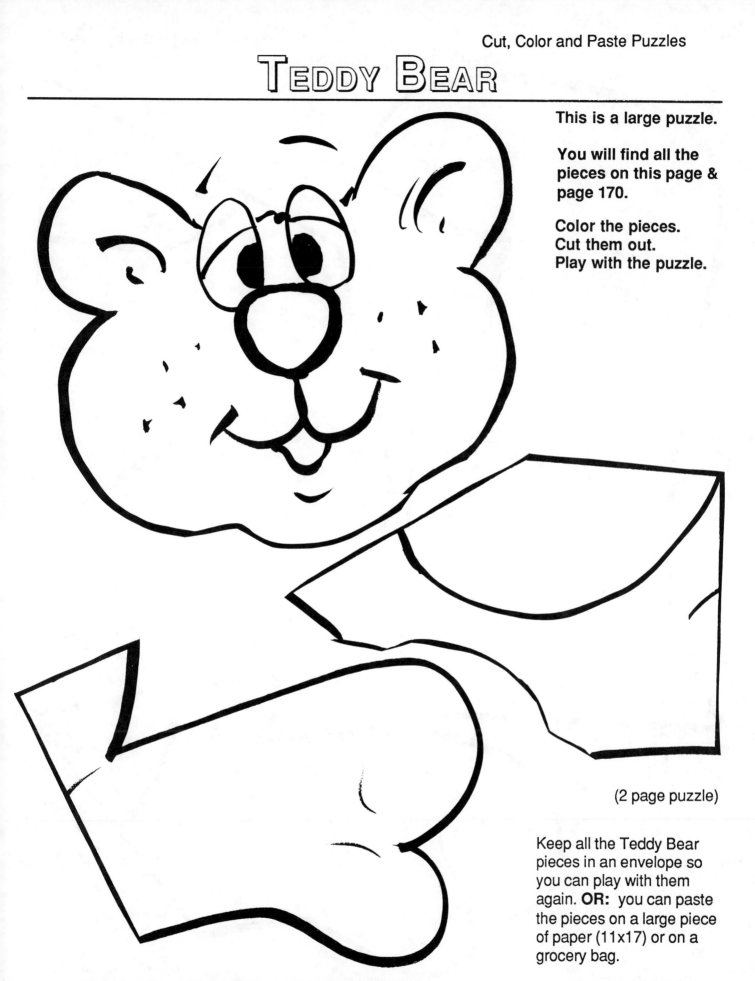

This is a large puzzle.

You will find all the pieces on this page & page 170.

Color the pieces.
Cut them out.
Play with the puzzle.

(2 page puzzle)

Keep all the Teddy Bear pieces in an envelope so you can play with them again. **OR:** you can paste the pieces on a large piece of paper (11x17) or on a grocery bag.

Teddy Bear Puzzle Pieces

A Story Puzzle

Color the picture. Cut along the dotted lines. Have fun playing with the puzzle.

Goldilocks and the Three Bears

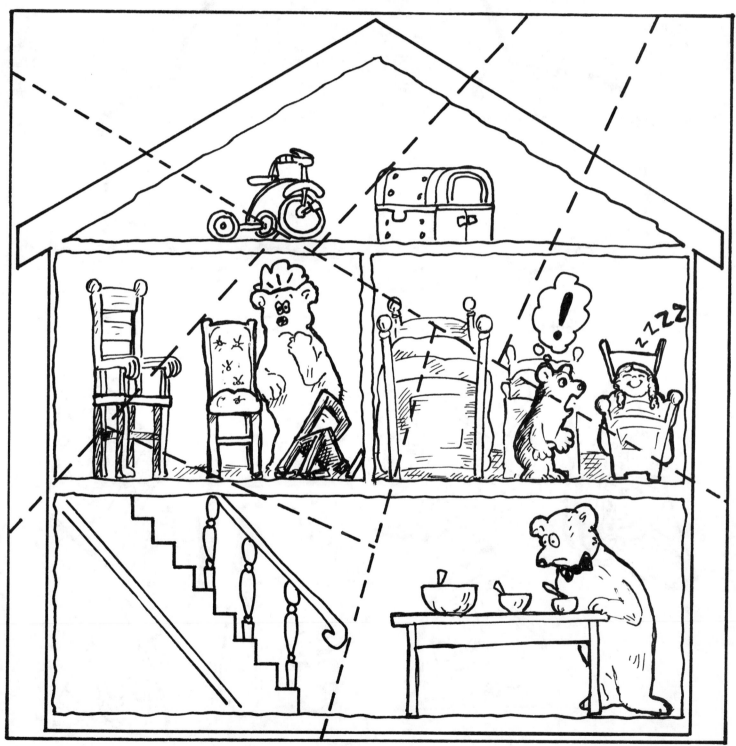

LITTLE CAR

Cut out the pieces. Paste them on the car shape. Color the car.

THE CASTLE

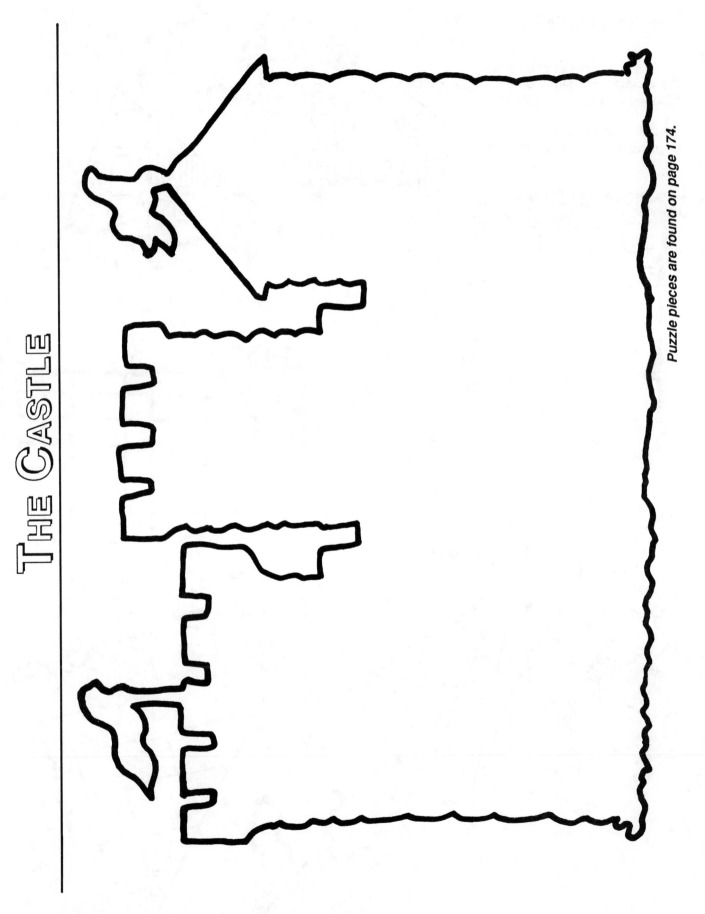

Puzzle pieces are found on page 174.

The Castle Puzzle Pieces

Cut out the Castle puzzle pieces.
Put the pieces together on the
Castle shape found on page 173.

Color the pieces. Save the pieces
or paste them on the castle shape.

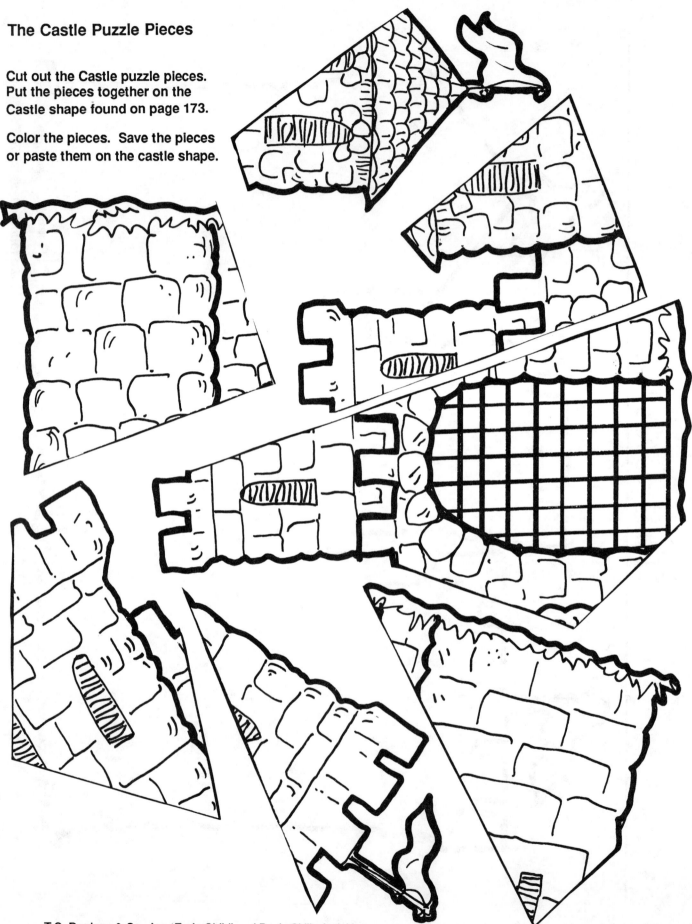

CHUG-A-LUG CHOO CHOO

Color all the train cars. Cut them out. Paste them on a piece of paper and you will have a very long train.

ROARING ROCKET

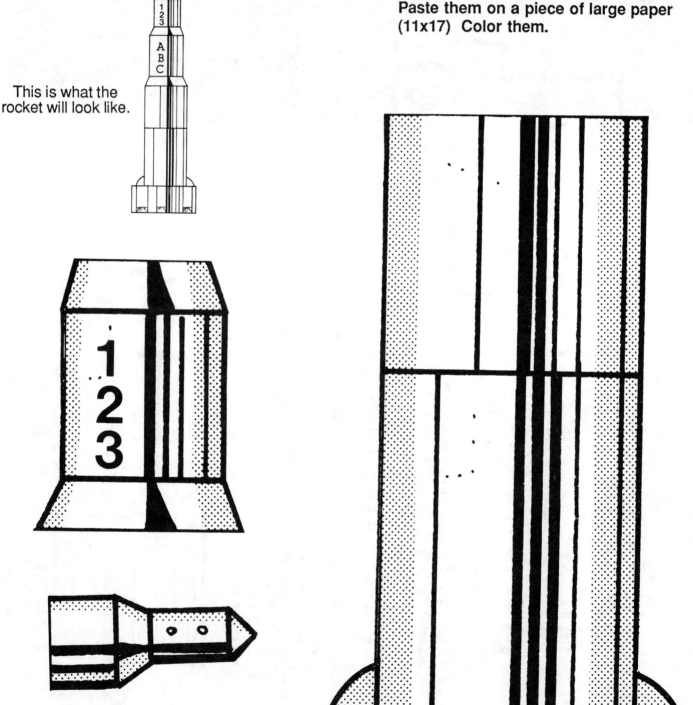

This is a large puzzle. You will find all the pieces on this page and page 177.

Cut out the pieces. Arrange the pieces. Paste them on a piece of large paper (11x17) Color them.

This is what the rocket will look like.

Roaring Rocket Puzzle Pieces

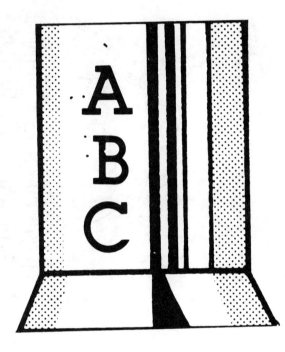

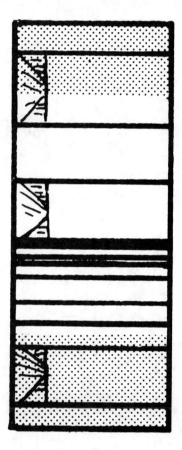

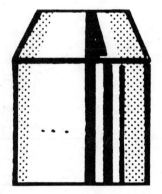

A STORY PUZZLE

Color the picture. Cut along the dotted lines. Have fun playing with the puzzle.

The Three Pigs

MORGAN MOUSE

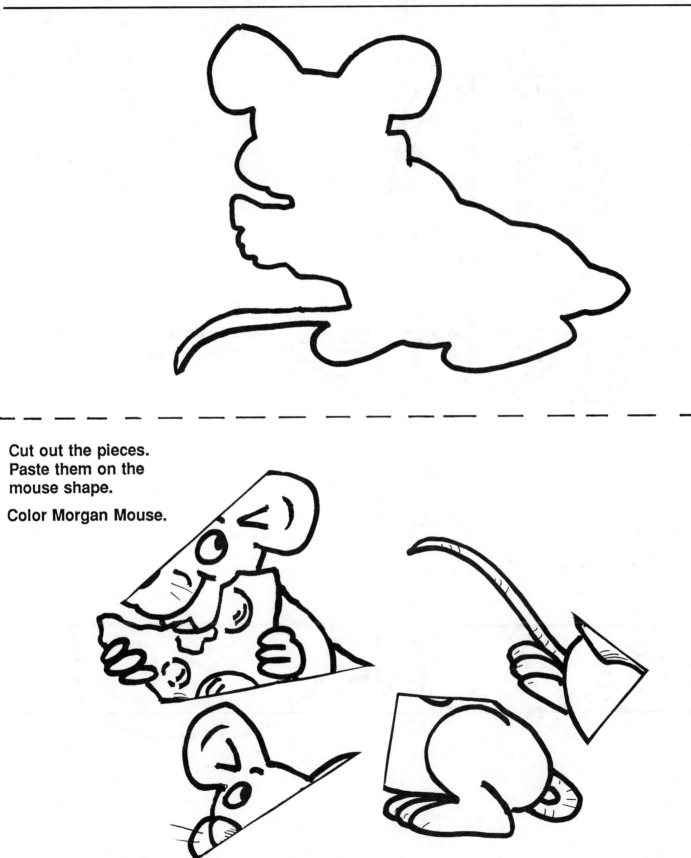

Cut out the pieces.
Paste them on the
mouse shape.

Color Morgan Mouse.

RANDY ROBOT

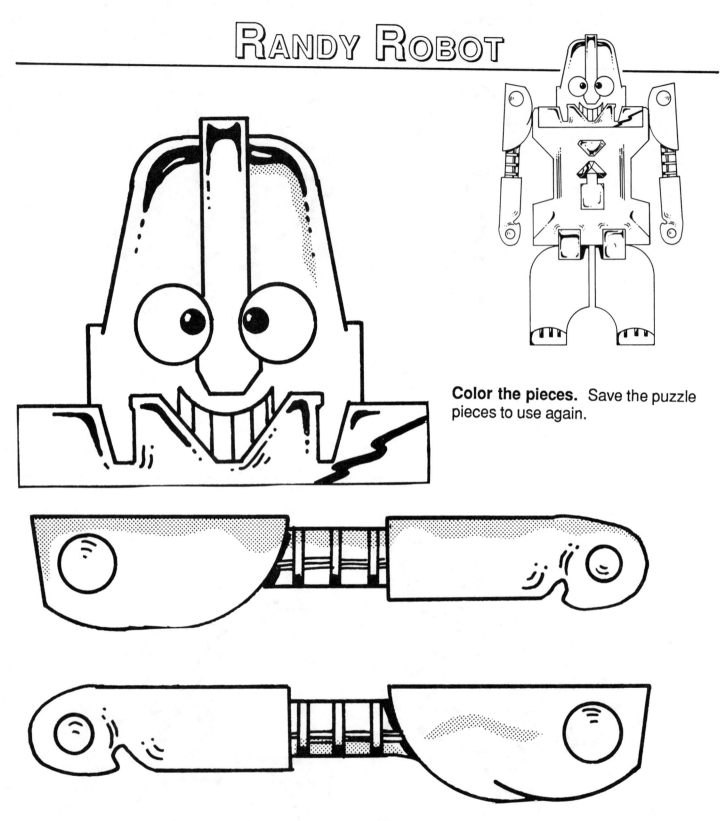

Color the pieces. Save the puzzle pieces to use again.

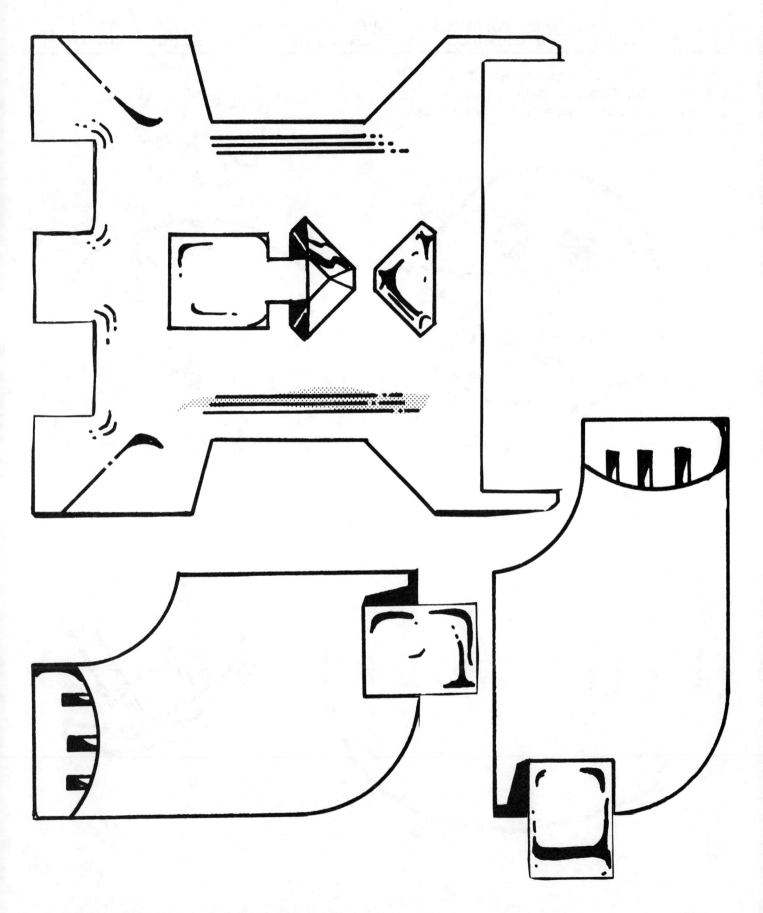

'SNOWFLAKE' THE SNOWPERSON

Color the pieces of the snowperson.
Cut them out. Paste them on a piece
of paper. Now you have made "Snowflake",
the Snowperson.

THE PERFECT PUPPY

This is a large puzzle.
You will find all the pieces
on this page and page 184.

Color the pieces. Cut out
the pieces. Play with the
puzzle.

(2 page puzzle)

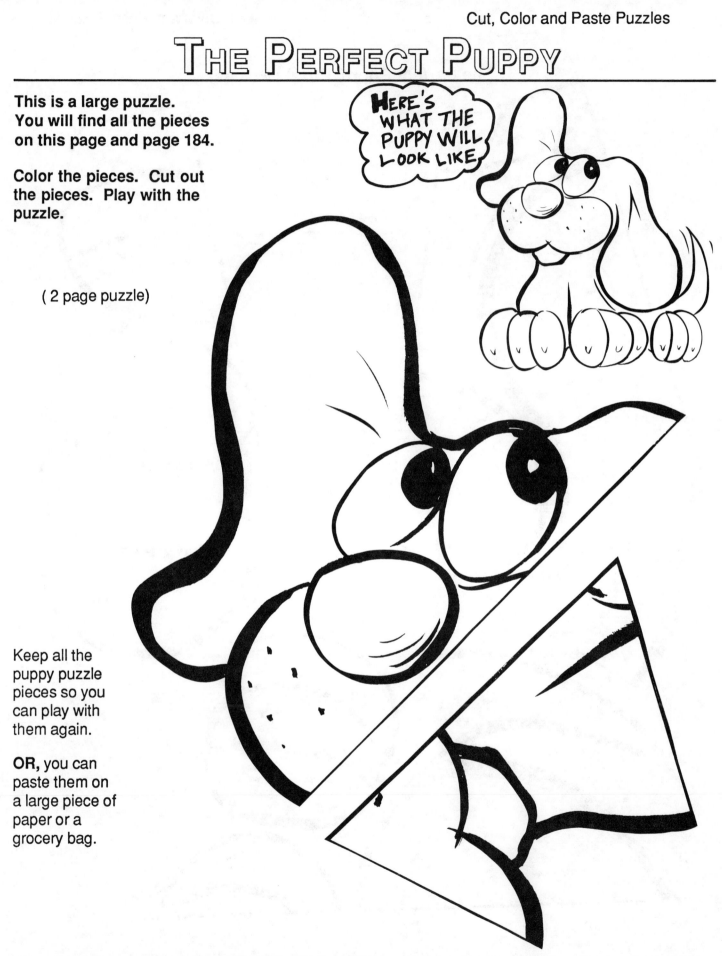

HERE'S WHAT THE PUPPY WILL LOOK LIKE

Keep all the
puppy puzzle
pieces so you
can play with
them again.

OR, you can
paste them on
a large piece of
paper or a
grocery bag.

The Perfect Puppy Puzzle Pieces.

_____

Child's Name   Date

has completed all the
Cut and Color Puzzles!

GREAT WORK!

Safety

Teachers and Parents,

The first few years of our children's lives, we are able to maintain a protective environment for them. We lock cupboards, keep doors shut, remove breakable objects, and keep infants and toddlers safe and close at our sides.

As our children grow and mature, their world begins to expand. The days of riding in shopping carts is over, the child-proof medicine bottles are no longer child-proof, they have learned to pick the locks, and they want to play outside alone. More freedoms are permitted in the neighborhood – from visiting friend's homes to bike riding. Children are curious. The world is a place for them to discover and explore. They want to test their independence. But at this same time, they may not always remember all the safety tips that we so diligently have taught them.

As teachers and parents, we should provide our children with some basic safety rules. These rules are not meant to scare children, but rather to arm them against possible hazards or potentially dangerous situations. Children who have had some training in how to handle these situations will find security and confidence in themselves.

The **Safety** chapter of *Early Childhood Basic Skills Activities* will provide children with the opportunnity to learn 22 safety rules. Each safety rule comes in the form of a coloring, cutting, tracing, or pasting activity. Performing a fine motor task on each page will reinforce each of the safety rules in a fun way. Each rule should be discussed and reviewed with the children.

On page 211, you will find a chart listing all the safety rules. After the child has learned a safety rule, he/she can put a star in the correct box on the chart. When the chart is complete, it's a safety award!

Stay By Your Parents

When you are out grocery shopping, at the park, at a shopping center, or anywhere away from your home, you should stay by your parents or the adult who is in charge. If you stay by the adults you are with you will not get lost.

Color all the people. Cut out the children and paste them next to an adult.

Obey Traffic Signs

Learn what the colors on the traffic light mean. And remember to look both ways when you cross the street.

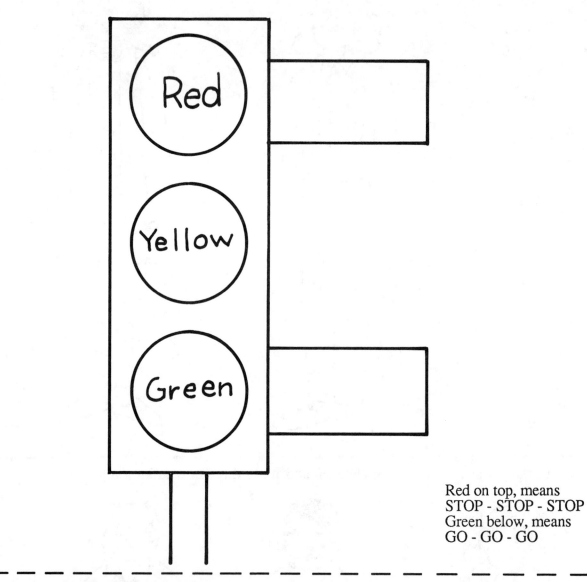

Red on top, means
STOP - STOP - STOP
Green below, means
GO - GO - GO

- -

Color the traffic light. Cut out the WALK and DON'T WALK signs. Paste them next to their matching color.

DON'T
WALK

Play Safe

Remember to share and take turns. Playing safe helps to prevent accidents.

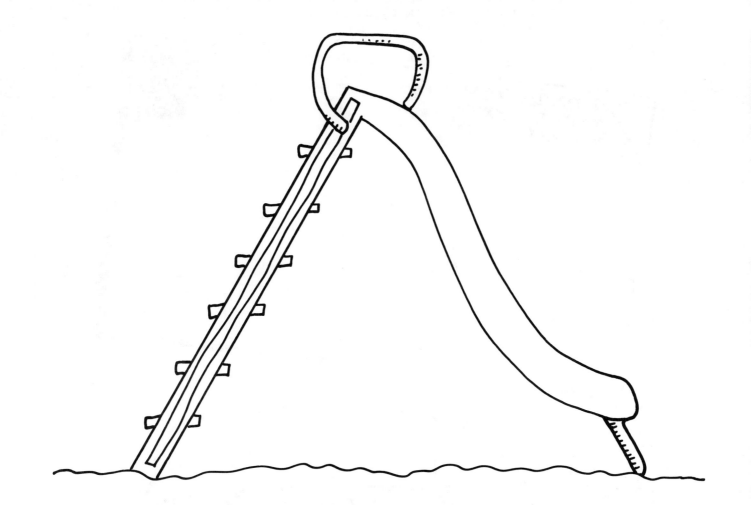

- -

Color the children. Cut the children out. Paste one child on the slide. Paste the other two children standing on the ground waiting for their turn.

Know Your Address and Telephone Number

You should learn your telephone number and your address.
If you were ever lost you could tell a helping adult.

Print your address on this letter.

Print your phone number on this telephone.

Know the Emergency Number 911
POLICE – FIRE – AMBULANCE

911 is the telephone number that you can call for help. Fire Fighters, Police Officers, and Ambulance Drivers can come and help if you call them. **Only call this number if you need help.**

911	117	111	911
121	911	911	119

Circle all the 911 numbers.

Color these people. They are all helpers.

Color 911.
Cut it out.
Hang it on your
refrigerator door.

DO NOT Talk to or Go Anywhere With Strangers

Strangers are people that you do not know. You should not talk to or go anywhere with someone you do not know. If a stranger (someone you do not know) wants you to go with them or wants to talk to you, you should walk or run away.

This child is walking away from a stranger. Good for this child. Color the child and give the child a happy face on this paper.

Tell Your Parents
Where You Are Going

If you want to go outside to play, or if you want to go over to a friends house, always remember to tell your parents where you are going. If you leave your home and do not tell your parents where you are going, they will not know where you are. Your parents will worry and you may be in trouble.

- -

Color the people. Decide where the child wants to go. Cut out the words and paste them by the child.

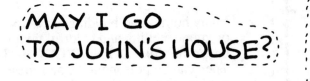

MAY I GO
TO JOHN'S HOUSE?

MAY I
GO PLAY
IN THE
BACK YARD?

MAY I
GO TO
THE PARK?

DO NOT Taste Anything, Unless You Know What It Is

You should not eat or drink anything unless you know what it is. There are many things that look good and smell good, but can be very bad for you. Ask your parents before you taste anything.

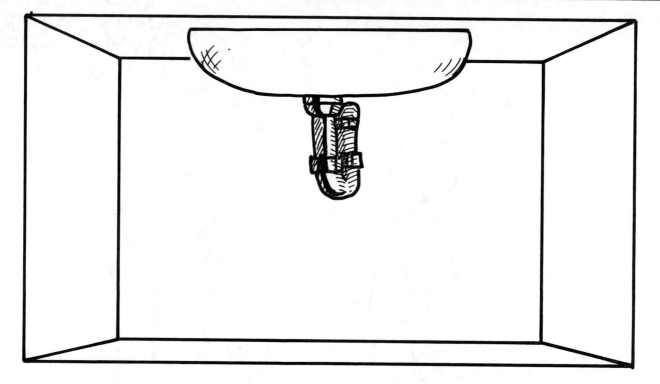

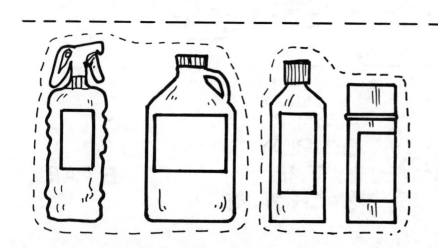

Many homes and buildings have lots of good smelling and colorful things under the sink. DO NOT TASTE THEM! They can be poisonous! Color these bottles. Cut them out and paste them back under the sink where they belong.

No One Should Touch
Your Private Parts

When your parents take you to the doctor for a check-up, your trusted doctor may need to check your private parts. You will need to touch you private parts when you take a bath or you may want to check your private parts. Your body belongs to you. No one has the right to touch you if you do not want to be touched.

Do you know what your private parts are? They are the parts of your body that are covered by underwear. Can you name all the parts of your body? Name the parts of the body on these children. Color the children.

Always Wear Your Seat Belt

Wearing your seat belt in the car is a very important rule. It will keep you safe in the car. When you get into the car, put your seat belt on right away. If the adults in the car forget to put on their seat belts, REMIND THEM!

This family is going for a drive. Trace over the seat belts in RED so you can really see them. Color the picture. It is SMART to wear seat belts.

Only Take Medicine/Vitamins From a Trusted Adult

The correct amount of medicine when you are sick can help you to feel better. Your parents or a trusted doctor will give the medicine to you. Too much medicine can make you very sick. CHILDREN SHOULD NEVER HELP THEMSELVES TO MEDICINE OR VITAMINS! Even if the medicine looks good and smells good you should not take it unless your parents have given it to you. If you find something that looks like a pill or medicine, give it to an adult right away. They will be proud of you.

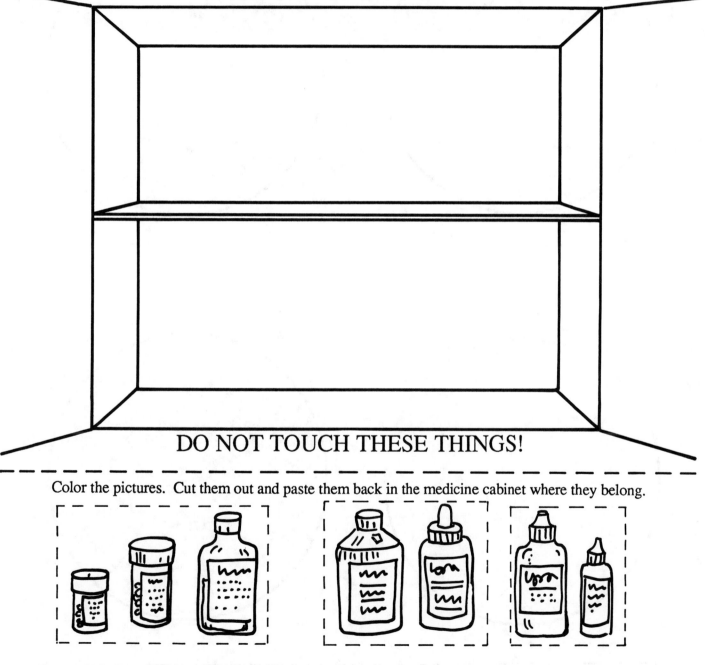

MEDICINE CABINET

DO NOT TOUCH THESE THINGS!

Color the pictures. Cut them out and paste them back in the medicine cabinet where they belong.

Who Can You Talk To?

People can feel happy, silly, surprised and even great! Sometimes people can feel mad or sad. When you are mad or sad it is important that you tell a trusted adult why you are mad or sad. Who do you like to talk to when you are mad or sad. Draw pictures of the adults that you like to talk to.

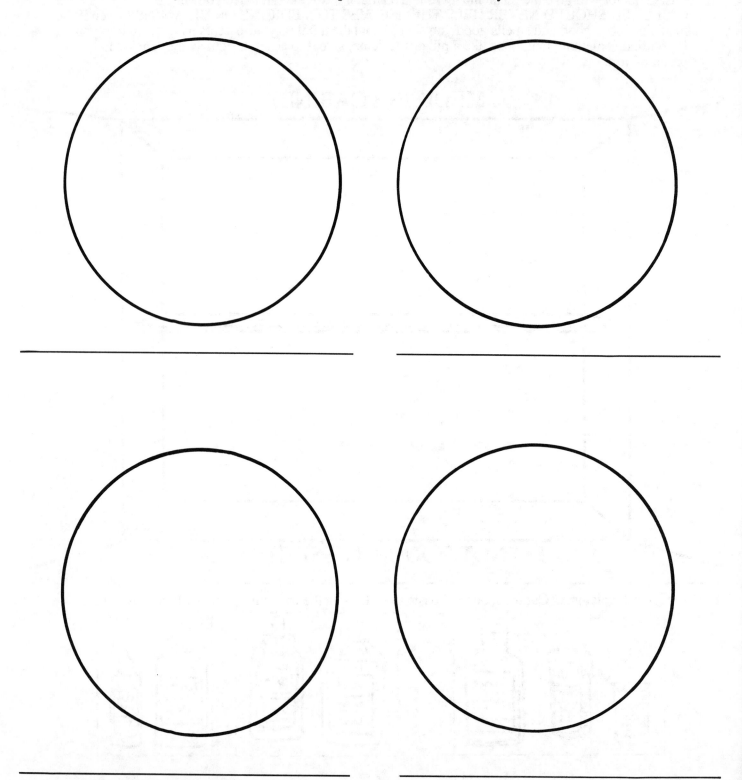

Beware of Animals
You Do Not Know

Animals are our friends. If you have a pet, you know how much fun an animal can be. BUT - You should not touch or walk up to an animal that you do not know. Even a nice animal when it is scared may bite. Also, remember, you should never poke, hit or tease an animal.

**If you have a pet,
keep it in your own yard.**

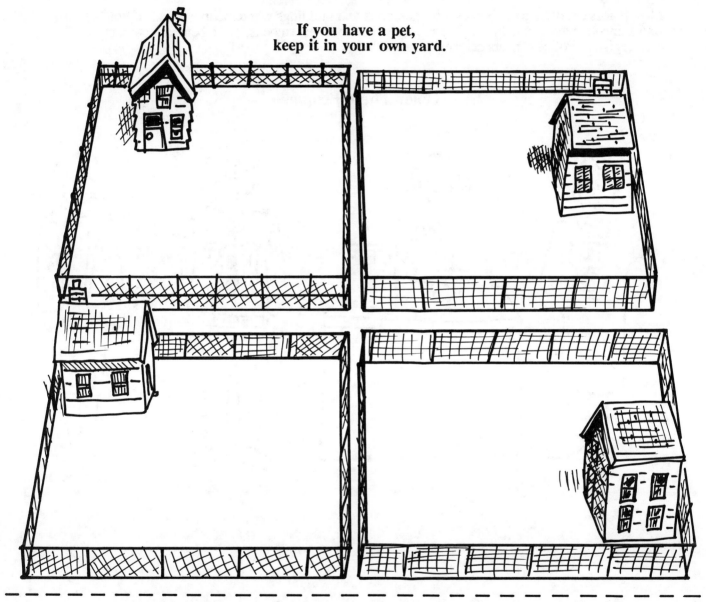

Color the pictures. Cut out the animals and paste them in their own yards.

Who Can Help You If You Are Lost?

You will probably never get lost because you have learned to stay by your parents, friends or teachers when you are out. But it is a good idea to know who can help if you do get lost.

Most places children go are stores, libraries, zoos and buildings where people work. If you are lost, find someone who works there. These people wear badges, smocks, stand behind a counter or a cash register. Police officers can help you too.

Color These People.

When you are out with your parents or teachers, talk about the people who could help you if you are lost. Point out these people.

Do not Touch Electrical Outlets

We use electrical outlets for plugging in lamps, small appliances and things that need electricity. Nothing else should be put into an electrical outlet because it could seriously hurt you. Adults should plug cords into electrical outlets, CHILDREN SHOULD NOT. The best rule to remember is not to touch electrical outlets.

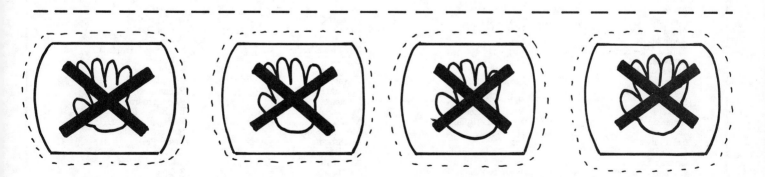

These are safety caps for the electrical outlets. Cut them out and paste them on the outlets, so children will remember not to touch the electrical outlets.

DO NOT Eat Unknown Plants

Many of the good foods we eat grow in gardens or on farms. These are good plants: beans, carrots, cucumbers, celery, lettuce, etc. Some plants that look good to eat are poisonous! Here is a list of poisonous plants. Talk about the list of plants that we SHOULD NOT EAT.

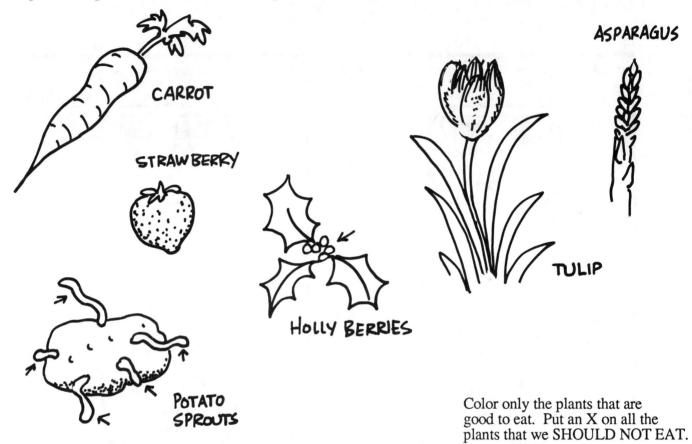

CARROT

STRAWBERRY

ASPARAGUS

TULIP

HOLLY BERRIES

POTATO SPROUTS

Color only the plants that are good to eat. Put an X on all the plants that we SHOULD NOT EAT.

Toxic

The following plants are considered **toxic** (poisonous, possibly dangerous). These plants contain a wide variety of poisons, and symptoms may vary, from a mild stomach ache, skin rash, swelling of the mouth and throat, to involvement of the heart, kidneys or other organs.

Acorn	Delphinium	Jonquil	Poinsettia
Anemone	Devil's Ivy	Lantana Camara	Poison Ivy
Angel Trumpet Tree	Dieffenbachia	Larkspur	Poison Oak
Apple Seeds	Elderberry	Laurel	Poppy (Calif.
Apricot Pit – Kernels	Elephant Ear	Lily-of-the-Valley	Poppy excepted)
Arrowhead	English Ivy	Lobelia	Pokeweed
Avocado – Leaves	Four O'Clock	Marijuana	Potato – Sprouts
Azalea	Foxglove	Mayapple	Primrose
Betel Nut Palm	Hemlock, Poison	Mescal (Peyote)	Ranunculus
Bittersweet	Holly Berries	Mistletoe	Rhododendron
Buckeye	Horsetail Reed	Moonseed	Rhubarb – Blade
Buttercup	Hyacinth – Bulbs	Monkshood	Rosary Pea
Caladium	Hydrangea	Morning Glory	Star-of-Bethlehem
Calla Lily	Iris	Mushroom	Sweet Pea
Castor Bean	Ivy (Boston, English)	Narcissus	Tobacco
Chinese Lantern	Jack-in-the-Pulpit	Nephthytis	Tomato – Vines
Creeping Charlie	Jequirity Bean or Pea	Nightshade	Tulip
(Ground Ivy)	Jerusalem Cherry	Oleander	Water Hemlock
Crocus, Autumn	Jessamine (Jasmine)	Peach Seeds	Wisteria
Daffodil	Jimson Weed	Periwindle	Yew
Daphne	(Thorn Apple)	Philodendron	

Practice Fire Escapes

You will probably never be in a building that is on fire. Just in case, you should know how to get out of a building that is on fire. Practicing how to get out of a building is called a "fire drill." Schools have fire drills. You should practice and have fire drills at home. Remember what your teachers tell you to do at school and make a fire escape plan at home with your parents.

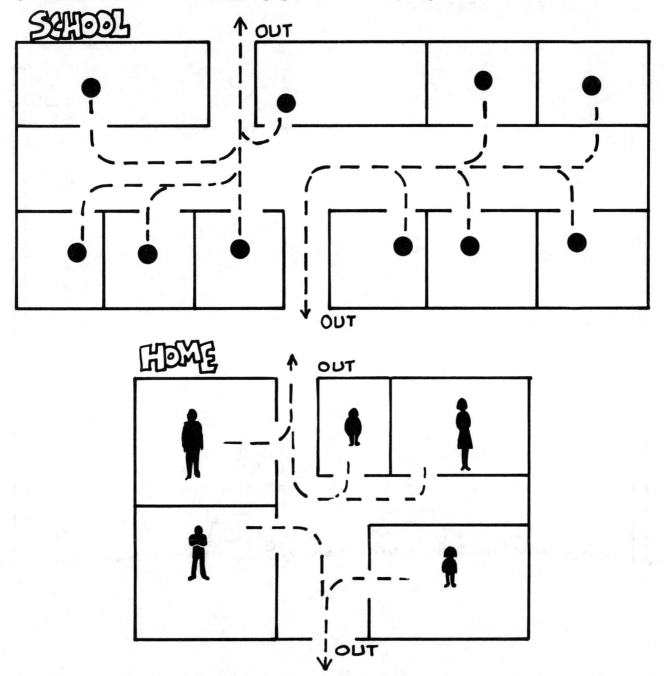

Here is a picture of a school and of a home. The dotted lines are the path that the people should follow for a fire escape. Trace over the dotted lines so all the people get out of the buildings safely. Both buildings have two ways to get out. When you practice fire drills, you should plan two ways to get out of a building.

No Kite Flying By Power Lines

Kite flying is fun, but can be dangerous if there are power lines near by. Power lines carry electricity. If a kite gets caught in a power line, it could be very serous and you could be badly hurt. DO NOT FLY KITES NEAR POWER LINES.

Trace over the power lines and color the children. These children are not flying kites by the power lines. They decided to play ball instead.

DO NOT Play In Water Alone

Water is tons of fun to play in. Lakes, oceans, ponds, rivers, swimming pools and bathtubs provide great fun if an adult is with you. Children should not get into water unless an adult is near you. Listen to adults and stay away from the water unless an adult is with you.

- -

Color the pictures. Cut out the adults and paste them next to each of the pictures of the children.

DO NOT Run Into The Street

When you are playing outside, there are many types of toys that can roll into the street. (Balls, wagons, bikes, frisbees, etc.) If a toy goes into the street you should know what the rule the adult in charge has set for you.

Older children may be able to go and get their own toy if they LOOK BOTH WAYS BEFORE CROSSING THE STREET. Younger children may need to have an adult go into the street to get their toy. Know what you should do. Whatever your rule is, YOU SHOULD NEVER RUN INTO THE STREET!

Color the pictures.
Cut out the toys and paste them by the children in their own yard.

Plastic Bags Are Dangerous

There are many different kinds of plastic bags: dry cleaning bags, shopping bags, garbage bags, etc. They look like alot of fun, but are very dangerous! Children can get stuck in a plastic bag. There is not any air in a plastic bag. You can not breath in a plastic bag. DO NOT PLAY WITH PLASTIC BAGS!

If there are any old plastic bags in your house, you should tie knots in them before you throw them away. If the bags are full of knots, children will not be able to get inside of them or put them over their heads.

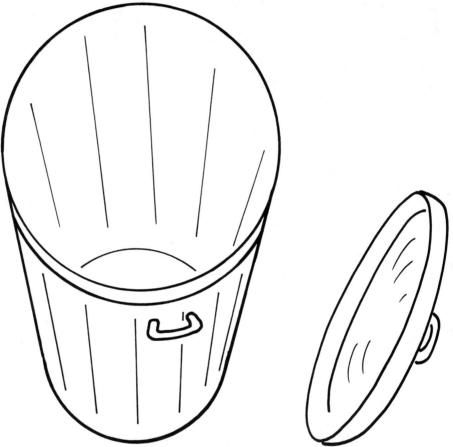

Cut out the pictures of the knotted plastic bags. Paste them into the garbage can so you remember not to play with plastic bags and that they should be thrown away.

STOP - DROP - ROLL

You have already learned about fire drills and how to escape from a building that might be on fire, but here is another very important rule to learn. STOP - DROP - ROLL. If your clothes caught on fire you should stop (do not run, it will make the fire grow), drop on the ground and roll. Dropping on the ground and rolling will put the fire out.

STOP   DROP   ROLL

- -

Color the pictures of the children. Cut out the pictures and paste them in order. Remember first you stop, then drop and roll.

Safety Rule Checklist

After each activity is completed – give yourself a ★ or ☺ in the correct box.

page 2 Stay By Your Parents	page 3 Obey Traffic Signs	page 4 Play Safe	page 5 Know Your Address & Telephone Number
page 6 Know the Emergency Number 911	page 7 Do Not Talk To or Go Anywhere With Strangers	page 8 Tell Your Parents Where You Are Going	page 9 Do Not Taste Angthing Unless You Know What it is
page 10 No One Should Touch Your Private Parts	page 11 Always Wear Your Seat Belt	page 12 Only Take Medicine/Vitamins From a Trusted Adult	page 13 Who Can You Talk To
page 14 Beware Of Animals You Do Not Know	page 15 Who Can Help You If You Are Lost	page 16 Do Not Touch Electrical Outlets	page 17 Do Not Eat Unknown Plants
page 18 Practice Fire Escapes	page 19 Do Not Fly Kites By Power Lines	page 20 Do Not Play In Water Alone	page 21 Do Not Run Into the Street
page 22 Plastic Bags Are Dangerous	page 23 Stop – Drop – Roll	*Great Work!*	

Congratulations to _____

You have completed the whole safety book.
You should be proud of yourself!
It is a good feeling to know how to . . .

STAY SAFE!

Places To Go

THE LIBRARY

GROCERY STORE

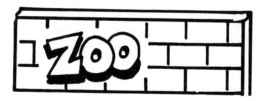

PLACES TO GO

To Teachers and Parents,

PLACES TO GO is a unique skill building book for young children. It will take your children on pretend visits to places that most children are familiar.

THE PARK	SCHOOL
THE ZOO	A MUSEUM
THE CIRCUS	THE LIBRARY
THE GROCERY STORE	A DOCTOR'S OFFICE
WINTER TIME	A CHILD'S ROOM
THE BEACH	

While the children are having fun visiting these places, they will be developing their fine motor skills, through the coloring, cutting, and pasting activities. They will also be enhancing their creative skills by designing how they think each place should look.

DIRECTIONS: Each "Place To Go" has been designed in this way:

- One background scene for the children to color has been provided for each place.
- One accessory page for each place, filled with all the objects and people that the children can color, cut out, and paste on the background scene.

SPECIAL NOTE:
Let the children be creative. There are no right or wrong ways to arrange the objects and people. The children should use their imaginations when deciding how they would like each place to look. Some children may even wish to draw in extra objects or people, or not use as many of the pieces that have been provided.

LANGUAGE EXTENTION:
Let the children tell you about their picture. What are the children in the picture doing? Is this "place" similiar to one that you have been to? What other things can you see at this place that might not be in the picture? What is your favorite thing in the picture? Why?

People and objects for THE PARK.

Color them and cut them out, then paste them in the park scene.

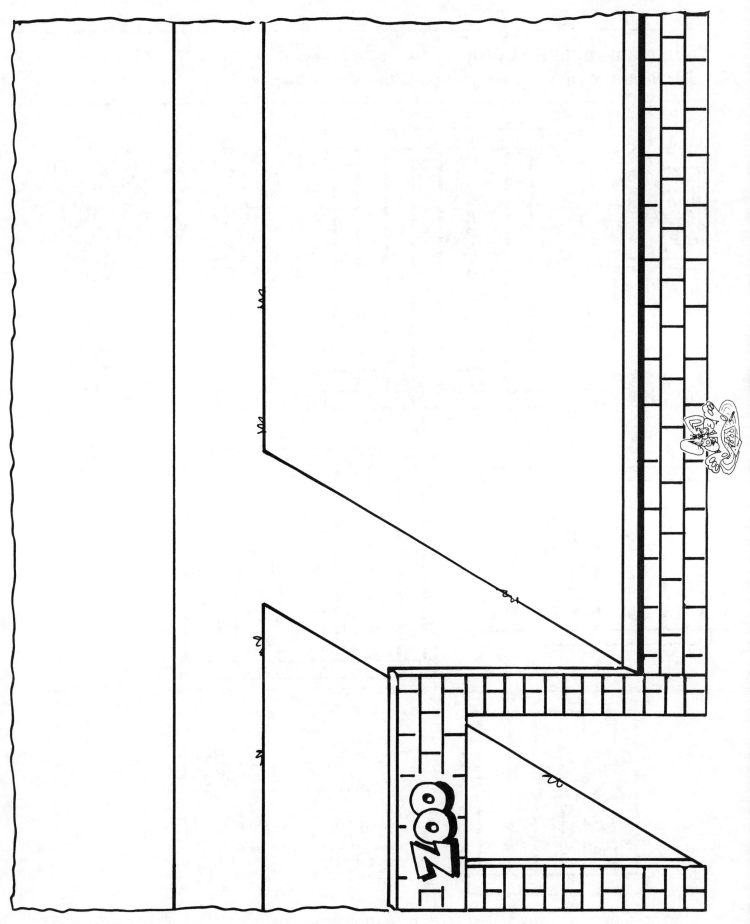

People, animals and objects for THE ZOO
Color them and cut them out, then paste them in the zoo scene.

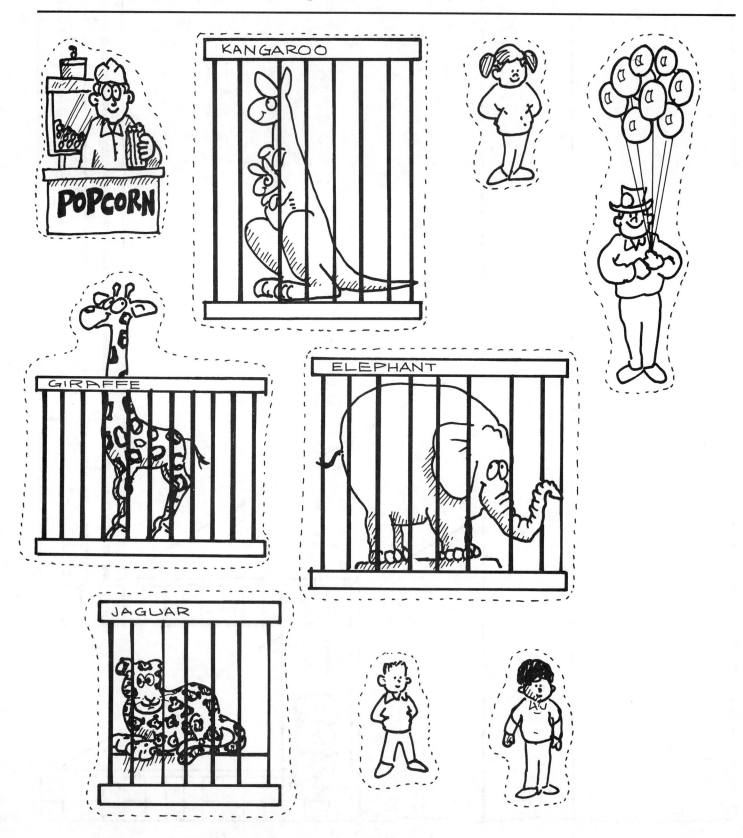

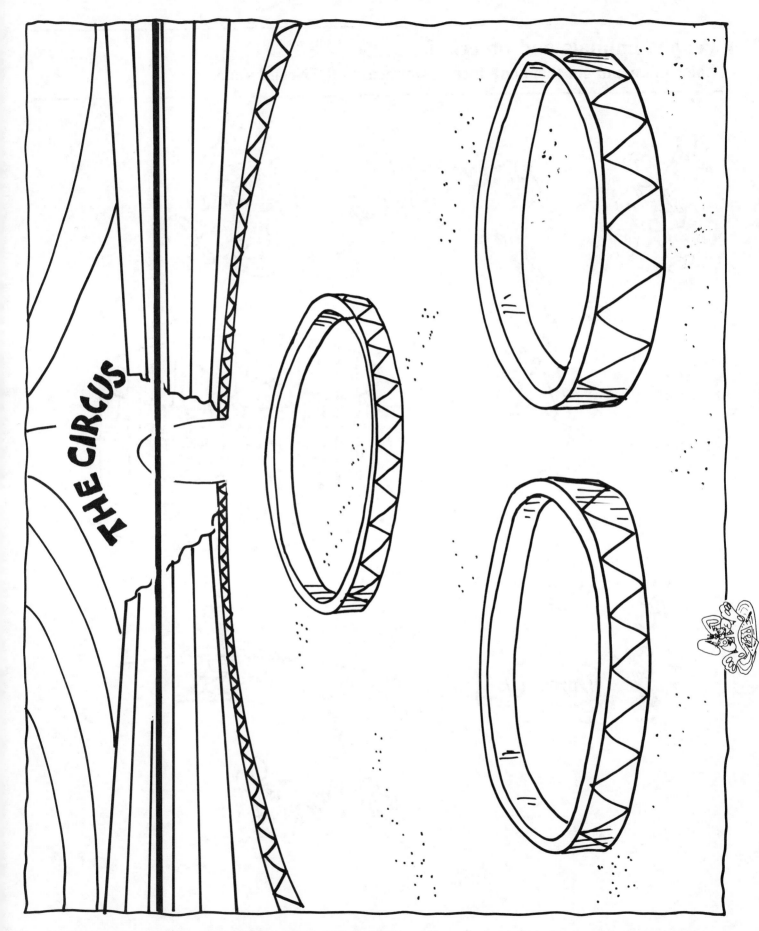

THE CIRCUS

People, animals and objects for THE CIRCUS
Color them and cut them out, then paste them in the circus scene.

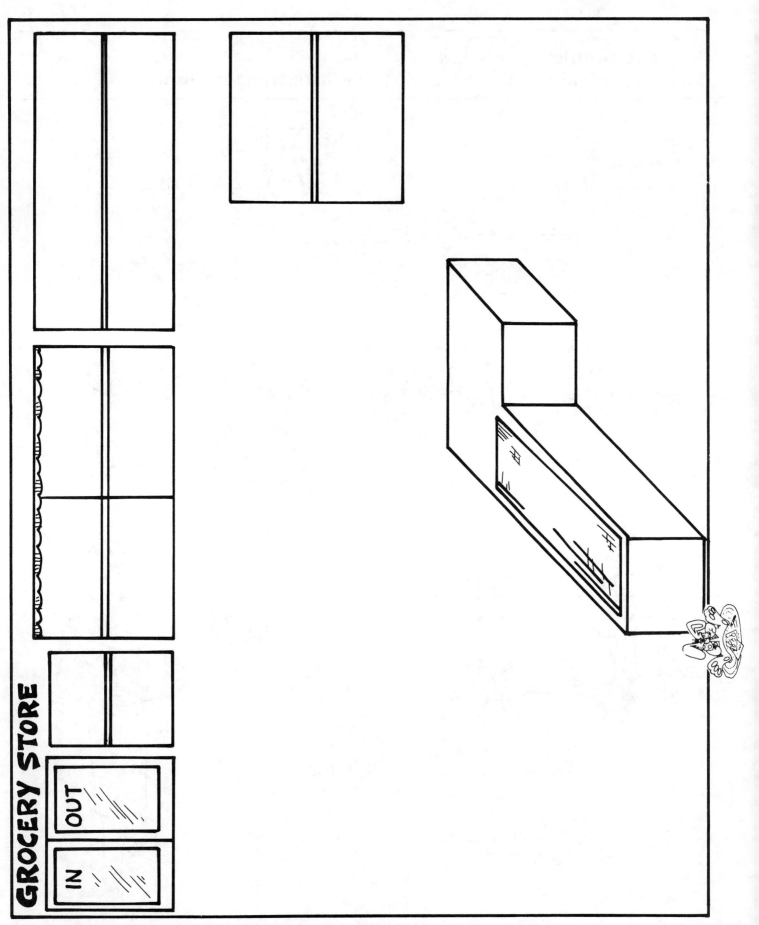

GROCERY STORE

OUT

IN

People and objects for THE GROCERY STORE

Color them and cut them out, then paste them in the grocery store scene.

WINTER TIME

People and objects for WINTER TIME

Color them and cut them out, then paste them in the winter time scene.

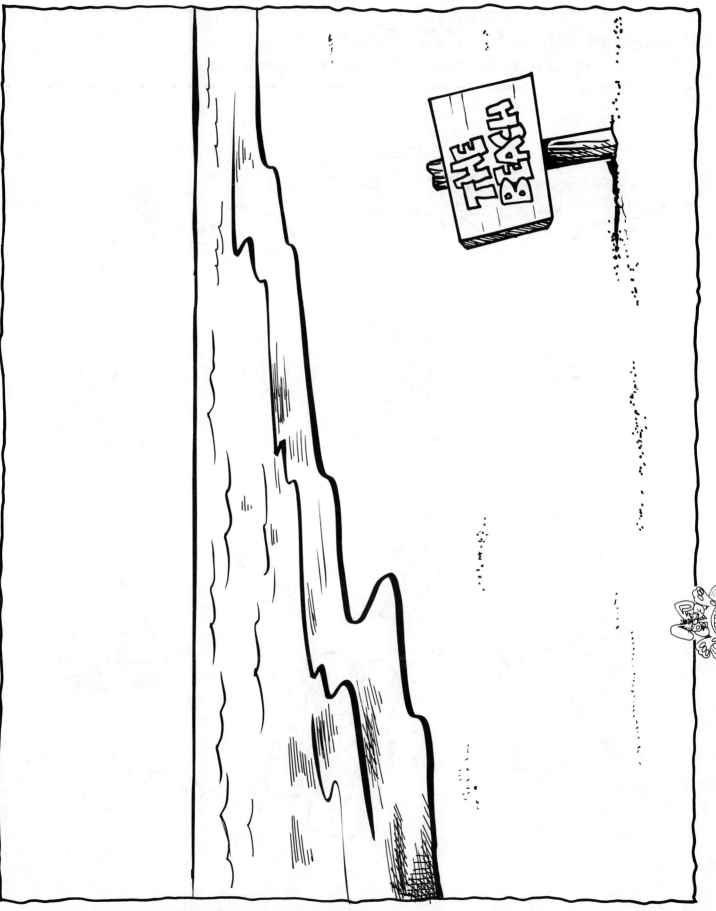

People and objects for THE BEACH
Color them and cut them out, then paste them in the beach scene.

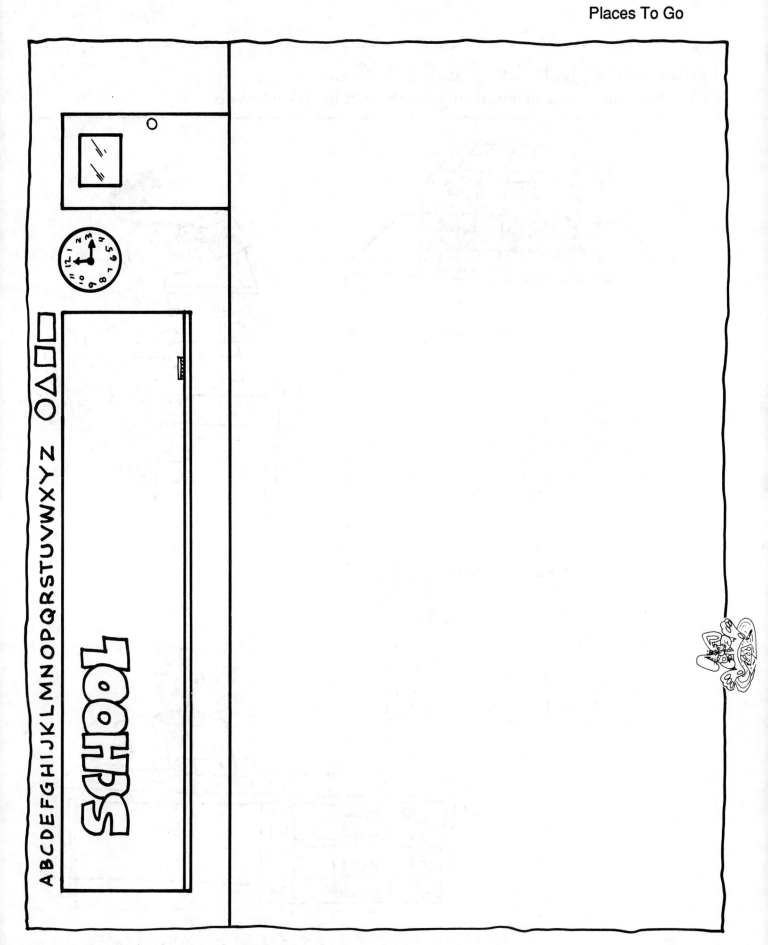

People and objects for THE SCHOOL
Color them and cut them out, then paste them in the school scene.

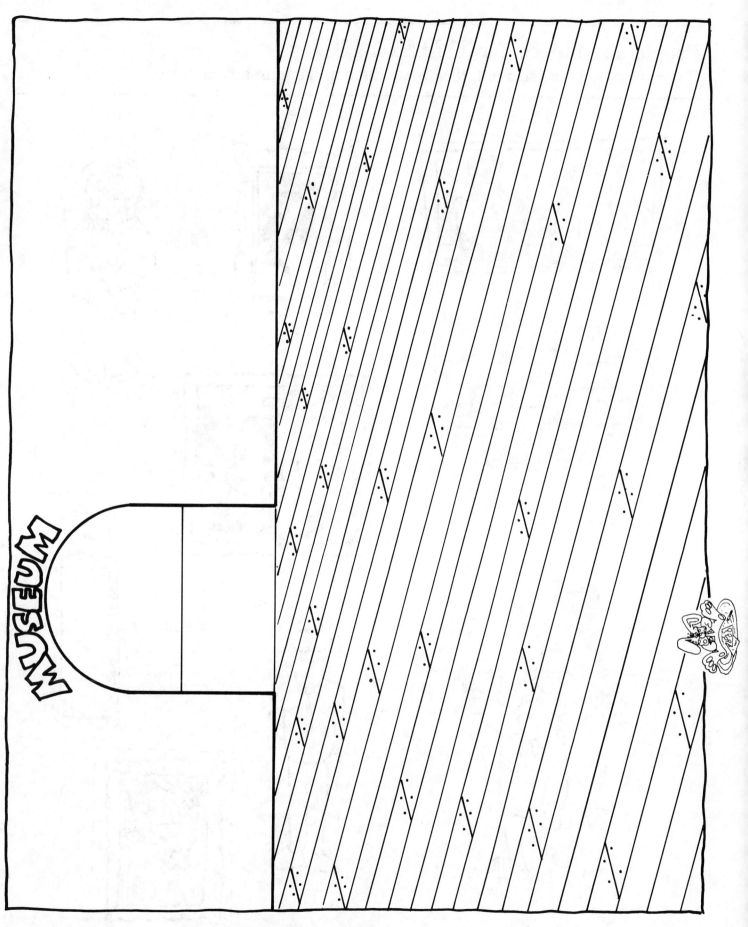

People and objects for THE MUSEUM
Color them and cut them out, then paste them in the museum scene.

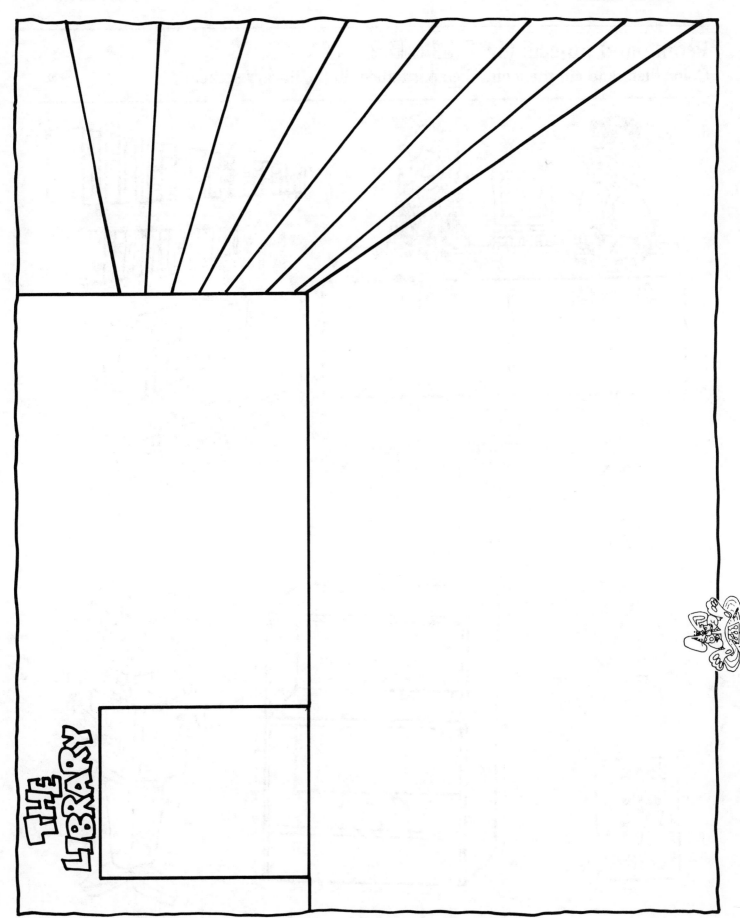

THE LIBRARY

People and objects for THE LIBRARY
Color them and cut them out, then paste them in the library scene.

THE DOCTOR'S OFFICE

People and objects for A DOCTOR'S OFFICE
Color them and cut them out, then paste them in the doctor's office scene.

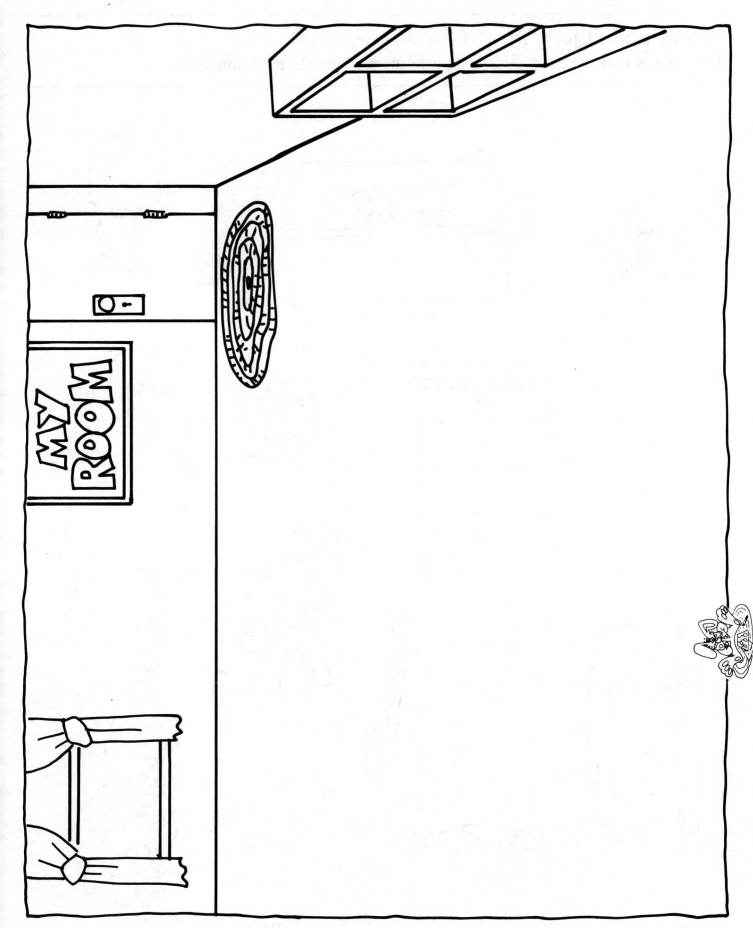

People and objects for A CHILD'S ROOM
Color them and cut them out, then paste them in the child's room scene.

TOYS

Visiting Places is Lots of Fun!

**Draw a picture of your favorite place to visit.
Color it. Tell about it.**

_____ *has finished the Places To Go
Teaching Tablet.*

IT WAS FUN!

Teacher's Notes . . .

Teacher's Notes . . .

Teacher's Notes . . .